DIY YOUR SMALL BUSINESS WEBSITE

A Beginner's Guide to Making a Website That Works

Angela Lehman

Copyright © 2022 Angela Lehman

All rights reserved. No portion of this book may be reproduced in any form without permission from the publisher, except as permitted by U.S. copyright law. For permissions contact: TheFitMT@gmail.com

Table of Contents

Introduction 1

WHERE TO BEGIN

Chapter 1 Picking a website builder 6

Chapter 2 Choosing your Domain Name 13

Chapter 3 Hosting your Website 22

Chapter 4 Logo and Branding 28

BASIC CONTENT

Chapter 5 Putting your Website Pages Together 40

Chapter 6 Picking Photos 54

Chapter 7 Navigation 62

ADDITIONAL CONTENT

Chapter 8 Online Gift Certificates 73

Chapter 9 Online Scheduling 81

Chapter 10 Social Media 92

Chapter 11 Blog 104

Chapter 12 Content is King – Beyond the basics 112

Chapter 13 SEO – Search Engine Optimization 121

Chapter 14 Review sites – Create an online reputation. 130

Chapter 15 How to get found online 141

Chapter 16 Paid Advertising 151

Chapter 17 When to hire a professional 160

Introduction

Welcome and congratulations on starting your own website! I was in your shoes in 2009 when I began my online presence with my first website. I had 12 years as a licensed massage therapist, a bachelor's degree in kinesiology, and 5 years teaching massage under my belt.

I thought, *How hard can making a website be?*

I was naïve. It was hard. Well, more time-consuming than hard. This book will take care of the hard part for you and save you time. You will save money or not spend money you don't have by doing it yourself with the roadmap I've laid out. Today, in 2020, after building my business to exactly the size I wanted it, I can look back and know it was difficult, but it brought me to this place of being able to help you reach your business goals.

In this book, I hope you'll find inspiration, guidance, and many fewer moments of "What the @_%#?!" than I encountered. I've shared hours of trial and error, years of re-doing and refining, countless failures and mistakes all in one easy-to-find place.

Are you ready to bring in as many customers as you can handle? Are you excited to be found on the web? Will you be kicking back with a mimosa feeling proud of your accomplishments? Yes, yes, and yes! After reading this book and complete the steps, you will successfully have an up and running website for your business with the tools in place for being found on the web. Come with me and let's get started building your website into a customer generating machine!

How to Use This Book

I present chapters in order of what to do first, and each subsequent chapter will build on the chapter before. I still think this is the best way to read and complete the activities in this book, but feel free to skip to the chapters you're most interested in and go from there.

Each chapter gives you an activity and note taking section. Then you can use the checklist to get yourself moving through this process, step by step. It won't be overwhelming when you take it one chapter (step) at a time. There is basic information on each topic, and I kept it basic for a reason. Often overthinking and an abundance of information causes paralysis! Basic works. There is just enough information to help you get it done and succeed.

Once your website is created and working for you, you can always make modifications and improvements.

You can always email me if you have questions. Please give me feedback about which way the book worked for you!

During my 5 years of teaching massage therapy and anatomy/physiology, I found everyone learns and absorbs information differently. I used this knowledge while writing this book and tried to explain things step by step and use as little technical jargon as possible. After all, we own a business and probably don't have time to become a marketing expert as well.

This book is for beginners of all ages. I had the challenge of bridging the gap between 20 somethings to 60 somethings, and we all know these age groups bring a vastly different knowledge base to the table on the topic of internet marketing. 😊

I'm telling my story as I would to a friend. I'm using examples from my business–examples that worked and didn't work. Use in order of chapters written at the beginning and then skip to the chapter you need when the time comes to develop that area more. This is meant for the beginner, the new to business, just starting-out group.

I am not a website designer, SEO specialist, or social media guru. I am, however, a highly trained massage therapist who put in the effort to build a business to the exact size I wanted and maintained it until I was ready to move on. I ended it on my terms, rather than going out of business because I didn't have enough business! When I look back on the 23 years of building my business, I'm amazed at how much I've learned. I know what worked for me, and I know it will work for you.

Are you ready? Let's make you a website that brings customers!

Disclaimer:

Prices change rapidly within online services for websites. At the time of writing this book, all pricing was current but may not be the same when you look things up. Understand this is meant to be used as a guideline, since there will undoubtably be variations as time passes.

If you purchased the digital edition, you may want to grab a pad of paper to take notes or work through some exercises. This book is in workbook format to take you step by step through the website building process. This is intended to avoid overwhelm and decision paralysis. I'll take it one step at a time with you, and before you know it, you'll be online and new customers will be finding you.

WHERE TO BEGIN

Chapter 1
Picking a website builder

We would all love to have the cash to pay a web designer to build a beautiful, state-of-the-art website and have our website show up on search results above our competitors. Realistically, though, we probably need to spend money elsewhere when we are starting out. Necessities like office equipment, computers, phone systems, client supplies, and inventory are a priority. Luckily, there are some good options other than paying someone to make your website. We are going to cover website builder products that help you build your own website. There are many choices for this website builder, and in my opinion, they all do a good job representing you and your company. These easy-to-use website builders don't require you to know code or have any technical knowledge about website design.

When faced with all the products out there to build your website, it takes time to sift through the options and decide which is right for you. I've done some of the legwork for you, presented it here, and picked my top three sites. I wanted to focus on free website builders but some will charge a nominal fee monthly. If a fee is charged, it is usually to get the site live on the web, which we will talk about in the hosting chapter.

Here is a list of free website builders:

- Go Daddy – easy to use and great tech support

- Jimdo – small online store builder
- SITE123 – great design assistance
- Square Space – best quality design features
- Strikingly – made for simple websites
- Weebly – ideal for small businesses
- Wix – best all around

My top three choices are:

- SITE123 – beginner-friendly with a focus on helping you get online
- Wix – it has a generous free plan and is easy to use
- Weebly – simple, stylish designs and handy tools

The beauty of these website builders is they have templates to walk you through the building process. I believe templates are very useful for the beginner. Some people say they limit you, but starting out, there is nothing wrong with templates. The main goal is to get the information about your business onto the web so potential customers can find you. These website builders will do just that.

> These easy to use website builders don't require you to know code or have any technical knowledge about website design.

Your website should reflect you. Your personality, your philosophy about your business, and your individual experiences in life create the one and only you. There are customers out there for all different personalities and business structures. You may be more casual in the way you dress at work, or you may be a dog lover and bring your dog to work every day. Depending on the type of business you own, your ideal client should be drawn to your business by the look and feel of your website.

Imagine a potential client wakes up with severe neck pain and goes to the computer in search of somewhere to get a massage. They may come across two businesses near their house, both with an opening that day, and pick one simply because it spoke more about how massage can help with neck pain than the other website, which they felt portrayed more general information.

Another potential client has her sister in town and they go to the computer to search for a day spa including massage. They end up choosing where they are going that day simply because they were drawn to the overall feel, including the colors and pictures used.

These two searches are going to bring up completely different websites. As you are building your website pages, have your ideal client in mind when selecting pictures, colors, and style of writing. Your website should reflect you but also should appeal to your ideal customer. I believe this is a benefit to building your own website. You have control over all the design options.

It's time to get started, and it doesn't matter which website builder you choose. All of the options listed here will do a good job of creating a professional-looking website. The first step is choosing one, and then the fun begins!

A word about WordPress: While WordPress can be downloaded for free, I haven't included it as an option here due to the complex nature of using it. There are many more user-friendly versions of website builders and which makes them better for beginners. I won't disagree that WordPress is a more versatile platform, but we are keeping it simple. Simple will sell.

ACTIVITY: Spend some time browsing the internet looking at different websites. It can be in your area of business or any other. Notice which sites you're drawn to–the colors, the font used for their wording, and the pictures. Whether they have moving graphics or video on the home screen. Some have music that plays when you get to the site. Simply observe and when you've looked at many different websites you will have a better idea of what you like and dislike to help build your website.

Notes and Research

CHAPTER ONE CHECKLIST

- ☐ Do the activity for this chapter.

- ☐ Do a Google search for "free website builders" or use the list at the beginning of this chapter.

- ☐ Compare the features of some of the website builders. If your business is primarily selling things from your website, there are some builders that are better suited to your needs (eCommerce) compared to a massage therapist looking for new clients to come to their business.

- ☐ Compare cost (if any) of the website builders you like.

- ☐ Compare template choices. WIX may have templates you like the look of the best. Remember that colors and pictures can be changed. Look at the layout to find something you like.

- ☐ Know your ideal client and keep them in mind while choosing a website template. The look and feel of your website should match the image you want your business to portray and attract your ideal customers.

- ☐ Pick your website builder and sign up for the free trial or just get started!

- ☐ Have fun! See you in chapter 2.

Chapter 2
Choosing your Domain Name

A domain name is the name-you-want-to-call-your-business.com. It's the URL, uniform resource locator. It's what people will type in on their computer to look at your website. Think of it as your real estate on the web. You are going to buy the best real estate (domain name) you can. This will give you an advantage even before adding SEO (Search Engine Optimization) to your website. We will cover SEO in a later chapter.

What makes a domain name a good one? Let's look at some factors that go into choosing a good domain name.

How to Find Out Which Domain Names are Available

If you haven't decided on a name for your business yet, this will possibly help you as ideally, your business name should also be your domain name.

Let's use a massage therapy business as an example. Many massage therapists use their own name and attach "Massage Therapy" or "Bodyworker" to the end and use that as their business name. For example, Mary Smith would name her business Mary Smith Massage Therapy. If that is the business name you want, you then look to see if MarySmithMassageTherapy.com is available to purchase.

There are multiple websites to search which domain names are available. The easiest is Go Daddy. You simply type the name of the website you want into the search bar (at godaddy.com) and it will tell you if it's available or not. This doesn't cost a lot as most domain names can be purchased for around $15-20 per year.

Is .com or .net better?

The .com website address is by far the most widely used, and therefore it may be harder to get the domain name you want as a .com address. MarySmithMassageTherapy.com might already be taken, so GoDaddy will offer you it for purchase as a .net or .biz or some other extension. MarySmithMassageTherapy.net will work, but let's look at the advantages to using a .com address.

Some say a .com address builds creditability and looks more legitimate than other extensions.

The .com address is easy for your customers to remember and will be the first extension they enter in the web browser. Even a not-computer-savvy beginner knows what .com is.

Let's take Sally, an older client of Mary Smith's, who saw Mary for one appointment. She took Mary's business card but can't find it and wants to schedule another appointment. She remembers Mary's name and goes to her computer and types in MarySmithMassageTherapy**.com**.

She gets to a different website because Mary's domain name is actually MarySmithMassageTherapy.**net**. Oops, someone else got your business. Yes, this may be a silly example, but it's happened!

Another good reason to use a .com domain name is most browsers check for the .com extension by default. So, if the client just types in Mary Smith Massage Therapy (with no .com or .net), her browser will automatically show her results for the .com address first. Yay for your business, because you have the .com address and Sally found you!

> The .com address is easy for your customers to remember.

Most Searched Keywords

I feel I'd be doing you a disservice if I didn't address the topic of keywords in your business name and website domain name. What do I mean by keywords? Key words are the most often searched words when a person is online looking for a business like yours.

Think about the last thing you looked for in your phone. Maybe you needed a tire repair shop near your house or a plumber to fix a leaking toilet. Have you ever noticed what you type into the search bar? The majority of people will type in the **item** they need first and then a **word to narrow** it down. For example, "**tire repair near me**" or "**plumber to fix leak.**" If we take this example to massage therapy someone might type "massage for neck pain" or "massage in lakeside" (the city where they live).

One possible way to pick your business name and domain name is using keywords. This may not be the most conventional way of picking a business name, but it sure helps with people finding you online and bringing in business.

Think about this. If you do sports massage in the city of Lakeside and know people looking for a sports massage in your area will most likely Google "sports massage lakeside" why not name your business Lakeside Sports Massage? Even better would be Sports Massage Lakeside. Remember, *most people will type the item they are looking for before the narrowing word.* If your domain name is the exact words they are typing, guess who pops up first on the Google search results? You!

Other things contribute to you being listed at the top of Google searches which we will cover in later chapters but this is a brilliant way to get a huge head start.

What Will Your Business Name and Domain Name Be?

Now that we've considered Mary Smith Massage Therapy as a business name and thought about how potential clients search the internet for businesses like ours, do we want to change the name?

Another thing to consider is short and sweet. Use the least amount of words possible to name your business most accurately. *Mary's Massage* is good but lacking specificity. *Massage by Mary* is better because the keyword "Massage" is first. No one is going to type Mary in the search engine, so can we make it better?

One of Mary's specialties is prenatal massage, so she chooses *Prenatal Massage.* PrenatalMassage.com is already taken, so she goes to MassageforPregnancy.com and it's available! She's got her business name, domain name and is on her way to building a website and brand for her company.

Massage for Pregnancy might sound weird at first to say when answering the phone or when someone asks you what your business name is, but it will quickly become just a name that everyone knows. Like Kohl's or Target, it doesn't have to mean anything other than a name. Also, this name doesn't mean Mary can't offer other types of massage, but it will bring in business for prenatal massage and her website should show prenatal information front and center as to not confuse potential clients.

ACTIVITY: Brainstorm possible domain names for your business. What is it within your business you enjoy doing the most? Do you have a knack for a particular aspect of your business? What are your strengths and who would you love working with every day? What type of customer would you look forward to seeing? What area or city do you live in? This is an easy way to bring in clients who live near your office as most people won't travel far to a place of business. A **.com** domain name including your city is brilliant for free advertising. Once you have a few word combinations, start seeing if any of them are available for purchase with the **.com** extension. Good luck and think outside the box! Giving yourself a possible head start to new customers is never a bad thing.

Notes and Research

CHAPTER TWO CHECKLIST

☐ Do the activity for this chapter.

☐ Do you already have a business name? Type your business name as one word with **.com** at the end into your web browser search bar to see if there is already a website using it. Example: MaryDoesMassage.com. If your business name is already taken as a domain name, use the information in this chapter to pick a domain name that's close and relevant.

☐ Brainstorm some keywords associated with your business and the customers you want to reach. Consider using these keywords in your business name and domain name.

☐ Pick your business name if you don't already have one. Consider using the information in chapter 2 (keywords) to pick a name for your business that will also be your domain name. It's great if they match!

☐ Get the shortest possible name for your business and domain name. Short phrases as domain names are fine if easy to remember. Example: MassageforPregnancy.com

- [ ] Go to GoDaddy.com to search for available domain names. You simply type the name you want into the search bar and it will tell you if it's taken or available.

- [ ] Buy your domain name. Congratulations! You now have real estate on the web.

Chapter 3
Hosting your Website

Web hosting is the way to publish your website and go live on the internet. A web host, or web hosting service provider, is a business that provides the technologies and services needed for the website or webpage to be viewed. When you chose your website builder, it had a template for building each page of your website, but you also need hosting to be live and have potential customers find you on the internet. Luckily, you don't have to shop much for website hosting and the builder you used most likely will offer hosting.

When you pay for web hosting, you get more than just a live website. Web hosting companies typically offer in-house technicians to make sure their clients' websites are up and running 24/7. Your website should load quickly for any customer on any device. All major hosting companies know this and make sure their servers are running at peak speeds. Plus, when you need help or troubleshooting while creating or making changes to your website, the web host's support team is available for you to consult. My host's tech support is available 24/7, and I used them (sometimes late at night!) whenever I got stuck and couldn't quite get the result I wanted. I've called for things like pictures not saving, content being lost (they recovered it), not knowing how to add a watermark, needing a faster way to add a special to all pages without opening each one and adding it manually, email not able to send/receive, and domain name renewal.

It's a great feeling when you have someone you can call to get it done for you or tell you how to do it. The tech support is worth its weight in gold. Luckily, hosting doesn't cost what gold does. Many basic hosting plans are around $15 a month. Some give you a small discount for pre-paying a year or up to 5 years.

Many hosting providers will also offer email accounts with the domain name, which makes for a professional-looking business email. Think about the difference in having clients send emails to marymassage87@gmail.com or mary@massageforpregnancy.com. This is congruent with the domain name Mary purchased and her business name, MassageForPregnancy.com. These little things matter for an overall professional look for your business.

> If a website doesn't load in 2-3 seconds, about 50% of internet users abandon the site.

Now that we've covered Website Builders, domain names, and hosting, I'd like to look at them together to give you an idea of the cost. Some website builders will include a domain name and hosting. This gets confusing because they say the website builder is free, but then you need to pay for the domain name and the hosting or some combination of these. The prices I've given are basically what the pieces cost at the time of writing this book. As your website changes and evolves, you may need things added like eCommerce or a built-in gift certificate sales platform. Rest assured the startup costs for your website, domain, and hosting are minimal and you can grow into the rest. This is the beauty of doing it yourself. It's super affordable! If we use $15 a year for the domain name, a free website builder, and $15 a month for hosting, you will have a website for one year costing less than $200 compared to $3000 to have one made for you. I think it's worth a shot to make your own website.

I'd recommend picking your Website Builder (which you should have already done in chapter one) to see if it offers hosting and then, if needed, looking elsewhere on the internet for hosting companies. A quick search will bring up many hosting services like GoDaddy, HostGator, and web.com. Your goal is a reliable website that loads quickly, so your potential customers get the information they need quickly. We've all clicked on a website, gotten tired of waiting for the information to load, and clicked back off.

If a website doesn't load in 2-3 seconds, about 50% of internet users leave the site. Assuming the person who is searching has a strong wifi signal, you don't want your website to load slowly, so make sure the hosting company is reputable.

ACTIVITY: How many devices do you have at home? A desktop computer, a laptop, a tablet, and a phone are all possible devices your potential customers will use to look at your website. Use as many devices as you can to look at a website you like. Maybe it's a website you came across while doing one of these previous activities. Does the website load as quickly on all devices? Is the content on the website easy to read on all devices? A good website builder and hosting company will make sure the answer to both of these questions is yes.

Notes and Research

CHAPTER THREE CHECKLIST

☐ Do the activity for this chapter.

☐ Look into the cost of hosing through the website builder company you chose in chapter one.

☐ How much does hosting cost per year and what is included? Is there customer support if you get stuck? What are the hours of customer support and are they available by phone or email only?

☐ Do you want to pre-pay for 2-5 years for a savings?

☐ Decide if you want an email account associated with your hosting service. If they offer one, it may be for an additional fee, but may improve the overall professionalism of your business.

☐ Sign up and pay for your website hosting.

Chapter 4
Logo and Branding

A logo for your business is not required, but I highly recommend it. Your logo will be a picture or symbol with certain colors that you will use repeatedly in all marketing for your business. It will be on your business cards, website, social media, letterhead, receipts, emails, flyers, announcements, pamphlets, brochures, rack cards, gift certificates, specials, packages, and signage. All print or computer communication with your clients should have your logo attached. The goal is to have your business name come to the customer's minds when they see your logo. If your logo has a picture with the business name, when seen individually or together your clients should recognize it as your business. This is Branding. Your logo is just a piece of creating your brand or your reputation in the business world. Look at the following pictures and my guess is you will instantly recognize them.

These brands are recognizable worldwide and your brand will be recognized throughout all your customers and surrounding areas in which you work.

How to Design Your Logo

Your logo will reflect you and your business, so think about what your business represents. Are you all business or do you have a more casual, sunny personality? Do you want color included or black and white only in your logo? Most logos have color and black and white options. The original Nike swoosh is orange but is shown in black and white here.

In choosing the logo for my massage therapy business, I hired a graphic artist to design the logo for me. I had a basic idea of what I wanted, and after explaining it to her, she came up with a few different options, one of which was close to the idea I had in my head. That was our starting point and after many tweaks and changes, the logo evolved into my final product and became the logo I used for years to come. I felt this was worth the investment to get a professional-looking product that was unique to my business, and I knew I would use it every day. The cost will vary, so look up logo designers or graphic artists in your area or online with sites like Fiverr.com or Upwork.com to get a quote.

Better yet, see if they will trade services.

> Your logo will reflect you and your business so think about what your business represents.

Story of how I chose my logo:

A client had given me a small gift, which was a set of hands holding a votive candle. The hands were resting palms up, one cupped inside the other. I loved the detail of the hands and how they were open to receiving but also supporting each other in a caring nature. This is how I see massage and bodywork. We are there as a professional to support our clients' needs. Then with caring intention, receive what their body is telling us through our hands to deliver the best results possible for that day. I told the graphic artist I wanted hands like this in my logo.

At that time, I was also beginning my study of yoga, and one of my favorite instructors would often end the class with a saying:

"May the light within me honor the light within you, and just as the lotus flower blooms beautifully from muddy waters, you too go into the world today to share your beauty. Namaste." I like what the lotus flower represents, so I asked to have that in my logo. This is the logo we designed, and I used it for many years for my company.

These are the three different ways I could use my logo. They each had their benefit, and I appreciated the versatility and options my graphic artist provided with these different versions of my logo. I decided to add the tagline "Medical and Sports Massage Therapy" for marketing. You don't need to use a tagline, but let's briefly discuss what one is.

A tagline is usually a short phrase that accompanies your logo. The purpose of a tagline is to quickly express your company's most important benefits to your target customers. Walmart has a good example of this.

When picking your logo, you can do something with the letters of your business name, you can have an abstract logo, you can use your favorite animal in some way, or you can do whatever you want! It doesn't have to have some special meaning. It could be a tree or flower or an athlete, there are no rules. You get to be as creative as you want here!

Types of Logos

There are different styles of logos, and one style may represent your business better than another.

Wordmark style is when the name of your company is used with a specific font to become your logo. Google and Coca-Cola are examples. Google uses a very basic block font, but each letter has a different color, making it memorable.

Lettermark style is used for businesses with longer names that may want to use initials or an acronym to shorten into their logo to make it easier for customers to remember. NASA and IBM are examples of lettermark logos.

Abstract mark is where an abstract picture or symbol can be used to convey the values of the business. My Massage La Mesa logo was abstract as is Adidas.

Pictorial mark is an icon or shape that is easily recognizable and represents your business. Twitter uses a bird for theirs. Target is another example.

Emblem or Shield mark is the business name enveloped by a picture or shape. Starbucks is an example.

Consider Color

In the marketing world, there are definite opinions about color and how it makes people feel, consciously or subconsciously. In looking at the psychology of color, some would say it matters which colors you choose for your logo and business. I chose teal for my logo because I like it. I don't remember much else about the picking process where color is concerned other than I didn't want it to seem too gender-specific and I knew I didn't want red! There are some great articles online about color in logo design so I'd advise poking around and reading as much as interests you on the topic. Out of all your steps so far, logo color isn't going to break your business. So have some fun, have your logo presented with a couple of different color options, and ask your friends and family what they like. If you see it and have the reaction, "THAT'S THE ONE!" then stick with that.

Above chart used with permission by Canva.com

Where to Get a Logo

There is an alternative to hiring a graphic artist to design your logo. There are many online logo makers or companies that will generate a semi-customized logo for you in minutes, and the cost is minimal. These logo makers cost anywhere from $20-$120 compared to $200-$500 for a graphic designer. By semi-custom, I mean you get to select a picture, colors, and font for your business name, and then the program generates hundreds of possibilities you can look through. You decide which one you like the best, and after purchasing it, make small changes until you get your final product. You download all the different formats you will need for different marketing, and you're off and running! This is a quick and desirable option if you don't know exactly how you want your logo to look. It can be used as a starting point, and with an average cost of only $50-$75, there isn't much risk involved. You will get a completely usable logo which you can take to a graphic artist in the future for specialization or changes.

You can do a Google search for "online logo design" to get started. You have the option to find someone in your area or hire someone online to design your logo.

ACTIVITY: Search online for logo ideas and examples. Is there a certain logo style you feel would fit your business the best? Notice what you like and dislike about the styles and colors of different logos. Soon an idea will form for what you want your logo to be! Have fun with this! This is an exciting step and having a graphic artist to collaborate with makes it even more fun!

Notes and Research

CHAPTER FOUR CHECKLIST

☐ Do the activity for this chapter.

☐ Your logo should represent your company. Look at colors and different styles to narrow what you want your logo to look like.

☐ Look up logo designers or graphic artists in your area to see their work and get cost. There are semi-custom logo generators online that cost a fraction of what a graphic artist will cost.

☐ See how many revisions are included in the price and which digital formats are presented to you at the end.

☐ Decide what your budget is for a custom or semi-custom logo.

☐ Decide if you want a tagline on your logo.

☐ Pick the colors and style of the logo you want and send it out the designer of your choice. It may take some time with revisions to come to your final product, so get started now.

BASIC CONTENT

Chapter 5
Putting your Website Pages Together

This is where you begin to use your website template to add information to the pages of your website. What you write is called content for your website. The basic content is important to provide information, to sell something, or offer a service. We are going to give examples of content for a business that offers a service, but these examples are easy to change if your business is not service-based.

What does your customer or potential client want to know? This is the main question to answer and will help you build your website pages. Put yourself in their shoes and think of all the information they will want before scheduling an appointment with you or becoming your customer. The top information people are looking for before choosing a business are location, price, availability, and if you offer the service they need. These items can be covered individually on their own page of your website. Let's say, for now, your website will only have five pages. Here's an example of how to include that information on these pages.

Home Page

I'm sure you've visited hundreds of websites over your lifetime to know the page that opens first is the home page or landing page. This is the first impression customers get about your business. Customers should see what they need to know somewhere on that page and get a quick feeling for your business. This is the page to put your best foot forward and make the customer want to stay on your website. Your business name and logo can be front and center with a picture of what you do. This page should represent your business and let customers know what you're all about within 2 seconds of looking at your home page. Another key point here is to have the most important information at the top of the page so your client doesn't have to scroll much to find it.

Remember, your website will be looked at on a cell phone frequently, and smaller screens mean more scrolling. Your address should be on your home page along with your hours of operation, phone number, and a way for the customer to schedule an appointment. A scheduling call to action may be "call us" or "schedule online." Let's use my massage business as an example. There should be a sense of the type of massage you offer or your specialty if you have one.

I revised my home page a couple of times over the years. For many years, it was a welcome message and a brief overview of our specialty. This gave customers the chance to know if they were in the right place or to keep searching for other massage businesses if we weren't what they needed.

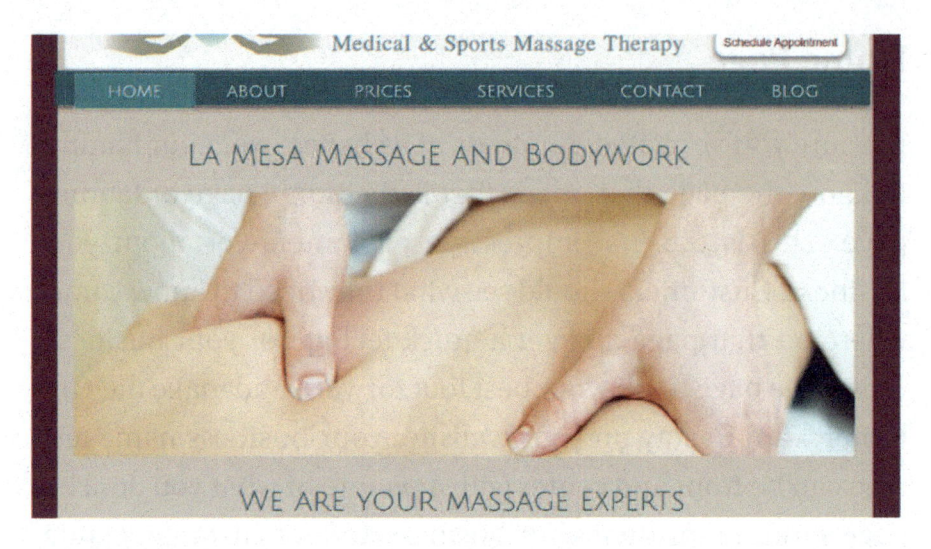

Another version of my home page was similar in that there was a brief "what we specialize in" and included bullet points of the conditions we had success treating. It had a "book now" button below each picture and title of the specific treatment. Sports massage, neuromuscular therapy, kinesiology taping, etc.

Other items you may want to include on your home page are links to your social media, online gift certificates, and online scheduling, all of which we will cover in later chapters.

About

This page is going to have more personal information about you or the business itself. If you are a sole practitioner, you could share what got you interested in massage, your education, or what area of massage you're most passionate about. You should add a picture of yourself as it is known to create rapport and connection with customers. This is also a good area to give your philosophy on massage and bodywork or your mission statement for your business. I've included a piece of my philosophy from my "About Me" page.

I believe the human body strives for wellness. The well individual is one that is happy, healthy, and whole and who perceives their life as one with meaning and purpose. The body needs to move every day in exercise and be fed a healthy whole-foods diet to remain functioning at optimal levels. Stress, injury, and disease begin to take over the body when the balance between body, mind, and spirit is not maintained. Massage is used as a way to keep that balance.

If you have a staff for your business, it is good to introduce and include a picture of each of them on this page too.

> When telling the customer about yourself, remember it's really about them. How can you solve their problem while telling about your passion?

Another piece you can add to the About page is telling customers how you're different. In my business, I only hired massage therapists with the highest level of education, and they had to have at least two years of massage experience. This was because the types of clients we drew were commonly post-surgical, auto accidents, and/or currently in physical therapy. I needed to maintain the trust of my referral sources. This set us apart, so I let it be known we had the most educated therapists who were current with continuing education so clients could rest assured they were getting a competent therapist.

Price

Your price page should be pretty straightforward. List your prices clearly for each service you offer. Decide if you're going to offer package prices, add-ons, other services besides massage, and if you want to offer gift certificates.

For example, if you offer a 30-minute, 60-minute, and 90-minute massage, list a price for each.

Decide if you would like to offer package prices. Some people like to offer packages and some don't. I love them. One, they commit clients to come regularly, and two, they make the whole check-out process faster because you aren't collecting payment every time. On the other side of that, there is a much longer time before the client pays you again, so use your money management skills.

I settled on a package of 3 or 5 sessions and quickly did away with the 10-session package. Experiment with packages to see what works for you. Usually, the incentive for the client is to get a slight discount for pre-purchasing sessions. List your package prices below your general session prices.

Add-ons could be aromatherapy, foot scrub, or paraffin wax, and list a price for each. If you offer complimentary services like red light therapy, stretching, or kinesiology taping, list those.

This is a good place to list your policy about refunds. Just put it at the bottom of the page so it doesn't detract from the info people are looking for most. You may also list the forms of payment you accept.

```
MASSAGE LA MESA PRICE LIST

Individual Sessions:

1/2 hour massage                                          $50.00

1 hour massage                                            $80.00

1½ hour massage                                          $110.00

Add-ons:
Aromatherapy                                              $15.00

Deep Muscle Therapy (Cryoderm Heat and Biofreeze applied to one body part)   $15.00

Kinesiology Taping (one body part)                        $15.00

Stretching -15 minutes                                    $25.00

Packages:
3 x 1 hour massage                                       $235.00

5 x 1 hour massage                                       $385.00
```

I prefer to give detailed information about your services on the "Service" page as I found customers immediately want to know what you charge and if still interested, they will read about your services.

The best advice I can give is to keep it simple. List your prices clearly and concisely with lots of white space around them so a five-second glance can give them what they're looking for.

Services

Now you get a page to showcase all you do. On your Services page, you will list each service you offer with a description to educate your customer. A nice photograph accompanying each service is optional but provides value. Think of yourself as the expert in what you do, and tell the customer why they need your service and how it can help them. This is where you may highlight your favorite service or the area you specialize in by putting it first on the page. If you like deep tissue work, for example, you can list it first with your explanation of how you do deep tissue, what conditions it can help, and why they should pick it.

A person new to massage may not know which session length to choose. You can educate them about the difference between 30, 60, and 90-minute sessions and when to use them. Many people don't know the difference between a Swedish massage and a Deep Tissue massage. You will list each modality with an informational blurb. This could be a couple of sentences long up to a paragraph. This idea holds true for any industry. Think about your services or products and what people need to know to make a decision.

If you have a service you feel takes more explanation, give it a page of its own! The more content the better! You may want to explain the way kinesiology tape works on the body or the common myths surrounding prenatal massage. The more information you provide your customers, the more they will trust you as an authority on your business.

> Building rapport and credibility is an important goal of any business.

If you run specials, you may rotate the special to the top of the Services page each month which also helps keep your website content fresh. Another advantage of building your own website is you have the ability and know-how to make a change as the need arises. This is a huge advantage if you would rather get changes made when you're motivated instead of contacting the person who manages your website and being at the mercy of their time frame. When you have a great idea for promoting a Mother's Day special, you can have it added to your Services page and home page within minutes. You will love this, I promise!

The Services page is also an appropriate place to include your policies about arriving late for an appointment, late canceling, or no-shows. Include them at the bottom of the page. You should also mention the forms of payment you accept. If you already listed forms of payment on your price page, it's never bad to list it again here. In business, I always say, "It's better to over-communicate."

Contact

This page of your website will include a "contact us" form customers can fill out and submit by email if they have a question for you. It will also show a map to your office, your street address, phone number, and email address. Your website designer will have a template for this page already done so you can follow their template, plug in your information, and there's not much else to do on this page! It is important to have this page as one of your easy-to-find buttons at the top of your website. It will get visited often and has a whole lot of information customers want in one location plus a map they can touch on their phone which will give them driving directions to you. Leave unnecessary information off this page so it remains clear and concise.

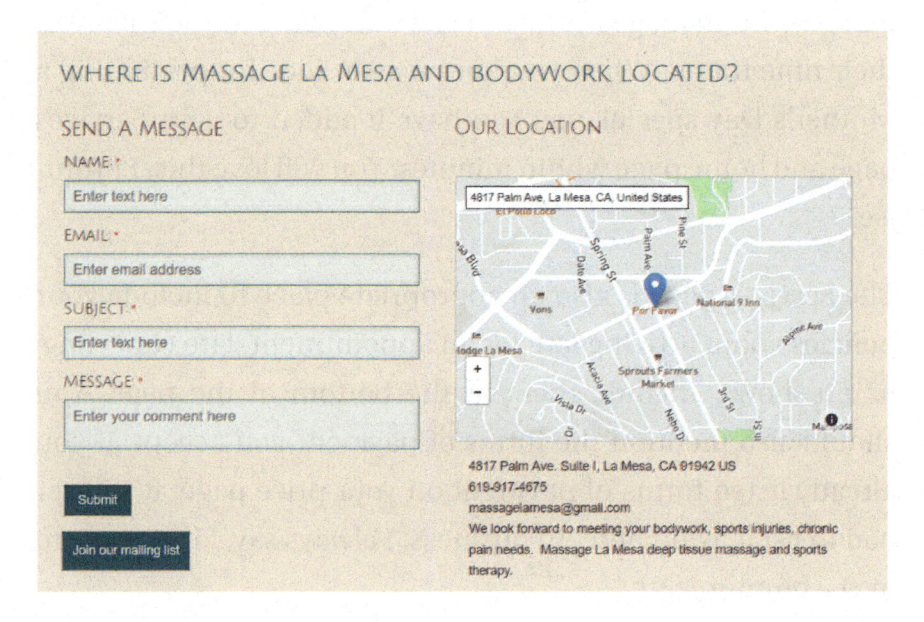

Availability

If you have a service-based business or need to schedule appointments, make it easy for customers to see where and how to schedule. One of the main things they want to know quickly when looking at your website is how soon they can get your service. Adding a "schedule now" button to each of your website pages will make your website customer-friendly and streamline appointments for you. We will talk all about this feature in another chapter.

It's time to build your first website pages! These five main pages I've used as examples are a guideline to get you started. Name your pages as you see appropriate and you are one step closer to having a live website!

ACTIVITY: Think about the examples given here and if they would work for the five main pages of your website. What main information would your Home page require? How would you like to present your About page? Are you going to tell your story in words or pictures or both? Include why you're doing business and how you can solve the client's problem. Do you offer services or are you naming the Services page something else? Do you have a price list you can put on your website? Some websites say call for prices, but depending on your type of business, deciding to not list prices can lose customers who think you might be too expensive or want to know the price right away.

If you don't need a Price page, what information does need its own page?

The Contact page will be used across all business types, so I encourage you to use a contact page.

Notes and Research

CHAPTER FIVE CHECKLIST

☐ Do the activity for this chapter.

☐ Identify what your customers or clients want to know. Make sure that information is on your website. Answer all the main questions like: hours, prices, location, and if you offer what they are looking for.

☐ Design your home page using the website builder. This is the place to make a good first impression. Viewers should know what your business is about within 2 seconds of looking at your home page.

☐ Design your "About" page. Tell customers about you if you are providing a service or about your business if there is a team. "About me" or "About us" are common titles used for this page on your website. Tell your story why you started the business or what makes your business different from competitors.

☐ Design a "Contact me" or "Contact us" page. Include the information talked about in this chapter.

☐ Decide the names of the other pages talked about in this chapter. Each page is listed with what should be included on that page so you can get started. The name of the pages may be modified to fit your business, but include all the basic information people will want to know.

- [ ] Make sure all information is easy to locate. Potential clients won't become paying clients if they are frustrated by your website.

- [ ] Congrats! You have your basic web pages written and designed.

Chapter 6
Picking Photos

As people visit your awesome website, they don't want to see page after page of words. Pictures add to the feel of the site and convey messages in and of themselves. Some websites might have more pictures than words, but a combination of the two will keep the customers interested in your site and hopefully have them calling you for an appointment.

There are different ways you can obtain pictures to use on your website. It's not as easy as grabbing pictures off Google images. Even if the picture doesn't have a copyright symbol, assume the image is copyrighted unless you know for certain otherwise. If you use a copyrighted image without permission, be aware the owner can take legal action against you. To avoid any messy legal proceedings, let's talk about the ways you can get great-looking images to make your website stand out.

> Stock images can be purchased or found for free from companies who provide them without having to worry about copyrights.

First, you can take your own pictures. Some people have a love and knack for photography and if that's you, great! If time is short or the types of images you have in mind aren't able to be photographed with your camera, then you can move on to the next option: stock photos.

Stock photo images can be purchased or found free from companies that provide them without having to worry about copyrights. The website designer you choose will most likely have some images available to you, and those are great if they work for your content. I found as I needed more specific images related to different services I offered (for massage) I had to look outside what the website designer provided. As you compare free images to paid ones, you may quickly find you like the paid ones better, or you may have to use them because it's the only way to find what you want. For example, when I wanted a picture of kinesiology taping for the Services page of my website, I didn't think my own pictures of tapings I had done with clients looked professional enough, so I chose to purchase this image from an online source.

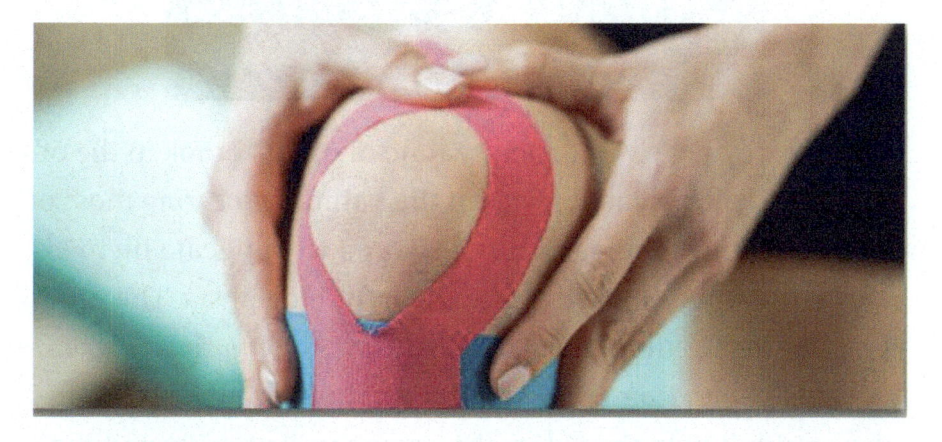

In the picture above, the background is blurred out and made all the difference. The picture below feels like it happened to have kinesiology tape in it.

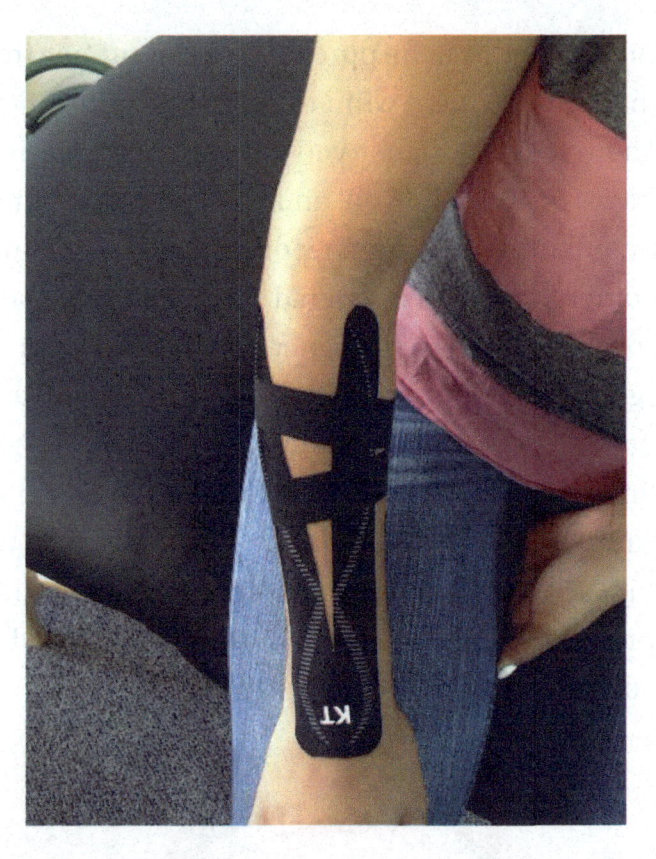

The picture above was a picture (one of many) I took in the office after taping a client. I was in the habit of picturing most of my kinesiology tapings in case I wanted to duplicate them exactly and because I liked to use them for blog posts. The problem with using them for my website was the variety of backgrounds depending upon where the photograph was taken. I also couldn't help the colors the person was wearing and their clothes often didn't look right on the page I was designing.

Another option is to hire a photographer (or trade services) to get specialized pictures for your website. They would be uniquely yours and not found on any other website like some free stock images tend to be.

One of my web pages had many different pictures shown on a single page, and I wanted some consistency to their look. By purchasing the pictures, they all had a white background and looked better together than if I tried to use free ones. Another good result of purchasing your images is they are yours to keep and use in other ways. I've used a couple of images I purchased for my website in print marketing material, special offers, and flyers for classes. Here are some places you can look for pictures.

Pictures for purchase:

www.DepositPhotos.com

www.StockPhotoSecrets.com

www.Shutterstock.com

www.iStock.com

Free images:

www.Stockfreeimages.com

www.Unsplash.com

www.Pixabay.com

www.Pexels.com

Whether you need general images for your business of massage, plumbing, bakery, or pet sitting, there will be many pictures available. The images are beautiful and will add so much appeal to your website. This part is fun and the finished product is worth the time it takes to select the perfect images for each of your web pages. Enjoy!

ACTIVITY: Search stock images or visit one of the websites listed above. Type in what you need to represent your business and look through the options. If you're not seeing exactly what you want, try going more abstract with the search or image. It's okay to think outside the box and use a slightly unconventional picture to represent your business. Just don't confuse people. Remember, your Home page is the first impression a potential customer will have, so be clear and show what your business does and they will know if they are in the right place.

Notes and Research

CHAPTER SIX CHECKLIST

- ☐ Do the activity for this chapter.

- ☐ Pictures provide information. Decide which images will enhance your website.

- ☐ Do you want to take your own pictures, hire a photographer, or use stock images?

- ☐ Search free and paid images to find what you need using the websites listed in this chapter. Remember, copyright laws prevent you from using most pictures you find by Google.

- ☐ Does your website builder offer some pictures to chooses from?

- ☐ Have fun picking images. They will help set your brand and the tone for your business.

Chapter 7
Navigation

Navigation is how a visitor moves around the pages and finds what they are looking for within your website. Navigation should be clear and simple so people don't get frustrated and leave your page if they can't find what they need. If a visitor is on your website and has to click four times to find your address, that is not simple and easy. You want to reduce your bounce rate by having an easy-to-navigate website. Bounce rate is the number of people who leave your website (or bounce) rather than continuing to view other pages. All the following information will reduce your bounce rate.

Navigation is important to understand because the purpose of your website is to keep people looking around enticed by interesting information, pictures, or great offers. You want to convert visitors on your website into clients, sales, or sign-ups for your email list.

> Navigation should be clear and simple so people don't get frustrated and leave your site if they can't find what they are looking for.

Visitors can enter your website from several different pages, so even though the Home page is important, the navigation from other pages on your site should be just as easy to understand and move through. Users should always know where they are, how they got there, and where they are going. Your website builder will include some features to keep navigation simple and easy to follow. Many website templates will include a header and footer that is shown on each and every page of your website. In addition, the main or primary navigation bar will always be shown. This automatically adds the clear cut where-they've-been-and-where-they-are-going aspect to the website.

Primary Navigation

Your main or primary navigation bar is most likely going to be shown horizontally across the top of your website. Another popular place for primary navigation is along the left side, running vertically along the page. When you chose your template, you will see this option for primary navigation bar placement, and if you strongly like one look over the other, pick a template with that look. There isn't much difference in performance between designs.

The primary navigation bar is where you will list the five sections of basic content we covered in Chapter 5. Our examples were "Home page," "Services," "Prices," "About," and "Contact," although you may have named yours differently. As this navigation bar is on every page, it increases the odds your visitor will always know where they are and how they got there. No matter what page they are on, they are only one click away from the next "most sought after" piece of information about your business. This is a good thing. Although it may be tempting to use cute and creative words for your primary navigation bar, don't! Simple, straightforward words leave less confusion with the wide variety of visitors your website will encounter.

I mentioned headers and footers and how they can be listed on every page of your website. This is beneficial because it will be another place you can add critical information about your business and have it always found easily. The main header mostly likely will include your business name and logo front and center on your home page. By having it as a header, it will also be shown on every page where someone may click. This gives your site a cohesive feeling and the person always knows the website they are viewing. Here is an example of a main header and primary navigation menu.

MASSAGE LA MESA
Medical & Sports Massage Therapy   Schedule Appointment

HOME   ABOUT   PRICES   SERVICES   CONTACT   BLOG

You may notice a sixth category here labeled "Blog" which we will talk about in a later chapter. Remember these titles for primary navigation are just a suggestion. Your website may require different categories altogether.

The footer can also be used to provide important information on every page. Even though your website may start out with five pages, after time you may grow it to many pages. I like to have the address, phone number, hours of operation, and a "buy now" or "schedule now" button in the footer. If your business sells gift certificates, you could have a button in the footer for that as well.

Basically, the most important "who" and "what" information, whatever that may be for your business, goes in the footer with your biggest call to action included. A call to action is what you want your customer or clients to do the most. Is it signing up for your email list? Is it make an appointment with you? Is it to call now? Buy now? Click here? This may sound like a lot to include in a footer, but if you space it properly, it works. Links to your social media sites can be here too. Many website builders will include this feature on each page so you may have it done already.

The following is an example of a footer. The call to action, "schedule appointment," is placed in the header and footer.

```
MON-FRI 10AM - 8PM        619-917-4675           Schedule Appointment
SAT 9AM - 3PM          4817 PALM AVE. SUITE 1
                        LA MESA, CA 91942
```

Secondary Navigation

Secondary navigation will usually be drop-down menus from the primary navigation bar. We've already created five pages of your website but most likely you will want more. The secondary navigation is where these pages will be placed. In order for the visitor to find additional pages not listed in your primary navigational bar, they can hover the cursor over one of the primary words and another menu will show. You've probably visited a website like this many times and your website builder probably already has this secondary navigation built in, so it won't be difficult.

Your job is to write content on the additional pages and then decide which area makes the most sense to place them. For example, if a visitor hovers on the word "Services," you may have an additional page dedicated to explaining each of your services in detail. This gives the visitor a choice to click on "Services" and read a brief overview of a service or click on the special service, like "Aromatherapy," from the drop-down menu to read about it in depth. We will talk more about ideas for additional content to add to your website later.

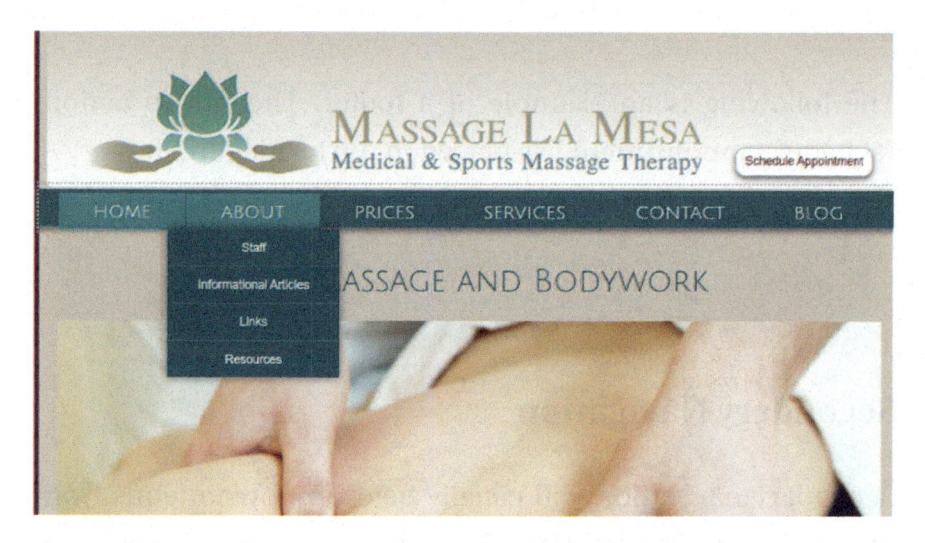

This example of a secondary navigation menu has a drop-down from "About" to additional pages on the website. Here a visitor could go to "Staff," "Articles," "Links," or "Resources." As you build more pages to your website, you will place them somewhere under your five or six primary navigational headings. Every heading doesn't need to contain a drop-down secondary navigation, but it is acceptable.

On my own website I had one or two areas which had a third navigational drop-down. For example, "Services" dropped down to a list, and when hovering over "prenatal massage," another menu dropped to a choice of two places to go. I don't love the third drop down menu, but sometimes it is the best way to keep customers knowing where they are going. We still want to remain 2-3 clicks away from all the information the customer needs, so getting too far into drop-down after drop-down increases the chances of them getting lost.

Navigational Pitfalls

Here are a few pitfalls to avoid when building navigation. One navigational pitfall is words that are too small to read. They may look good to your eyes, but what about the 82-year-old customer? If possible, have the words big enough to be read comfortably from arm distance away.

Another pitfall is using font that isn't legible. Some script fonts may be your favorite, but if visitors can't easily understand your words, there is a chance you will lose them to frustration. Keep the font simple.

This next pitfall I see a lot. Some people have scrolling pictures across the header or homepage of their website. While it may look high tech, think about the color of the words in that area to be sure they can be read as each picture comes viewable on the screen. If you've chosen black lettering and a dark background picture scrolls through, all of a sudden, your words can't be seen! That is, until the next lighter background picture comes up, but who wants to read your website in pieces? That's not user friendly.

The color of your font will be changeable in your website builder. Don't be afraid to use other color font besides black. If there is an area which requires a dark background, change the font to white. As long as there is strong contrast, your words will be easily read. It's perfectly acceptable to have different colored font in different areas. Again, "keep it simple" is the motto for website navigation. Present the information clearly and concisely, and you will have happy customers.

ACTIVITY: When your navigation is completed, have friends and family members visit your website and click on every page. This is a navigational proofread of sorts. Pick different age groups of friends and family, and the more honest they are the better. Get feedback about how fast the pages and pictures load. Did they find everything in an easy-to-follow layout or did some pages not make sense where they were placed? Was all important information clearly displayed on multiple pages? Can all font-type be read easily with good color and size of lettering? Are all clickable links live?

Notes and Research

CHAPTER SEVEN CHECKLIST

☐ Create clear, easy to use navigation for the main five pages you created in chapter five. The examples from that chapter were, "Home page, Services, Prices, About, and Contact. "

☐ Avoid cute and creative words for your page names. Keep it simple, straightforward and descriptive so visitors know where to click.

☐ Decide if you want a Footer and what information will go in it.

☐ Do you have additional information for your website, beyond the basic five pages? This information will go on a new page and into the secondary navigation. Decide where to put it.

☐ Your goal for all navigation is to stay 2-3 clicks away from all the information a customer needs. Customers should always know where they are and how they got there.

☐ Complete the activity for this chapter.

ADDITIONAL CONTENT

Chapter 8
Online Gift Certificates

Now that you've mastered your basic content, we can move on to adding more content to your website. The first area of additional content is gift certificates. If you are a service-based business, think about offering online gift certificates. In the spa and health service industry, this is common-place. Other businesses that aren't service based can still offer gift certificates. Whether you sell cupcakes or teach yoga or offer pet sitting services, you can sell gift certificates. An esthetician obviously would want to sell gift certificates, and everyone does from their office. They should also sell those gift certificates online.

For the little effort it takes to set up online gift certificate sales, the monetary reward can be huge. There are sites who specialize in gift certificates, and for a fee, you can add their sales platform to your website. I'll use my experience with The Gift Card Café to explain how I set up online sales of gift certificates for my website. There are many businesses like the one I used, so search online or ask a colleague who they use. After you sign up for an account, they walk you through step-by-step how to add a sales button to your website. You can customize the look and placement of the button.

How It Works

When a customer buys a gift certificate from your site, they get it instantly and can email it to the recipient with a message. How great and hands off for you is that? The Gift Card Café takes a percentage of your sale price, but for businesses starting out, this works because there is no monthly payment or commitment. You only pay when someone purchases a gift certificate.

After a while, I realized I needed to change the online gift certificate prices to minimize the hit to my bottom line from the percentage I paid for each sale. This was especially true for packages which were already discounted. By the time I paid the percentage for the gift certificate sale, I wasn't making what I wanted for each session in the package.

This led me to add a "convenience fee" where I raised the price for online Gift Certificate purchases. So, in the office a gift certificate was $80 but online it was $84. Many purchasers were out of state buying a gift for someone who lived near my business. This also was the reason my business name Massage La Mesa did so well online selling gift certificates.

Guess what the out-of-staters Googled when looking for a massage gift for Aunt Mary who lives in the city of La Mesa? They didn't even have to type the city, La Mesa, as the exact location for my business to pop up. We will talk about that more in the SEO chapter. Having an additional stream of income for your business is always nice and even better when you aren't doing anything for it. Your website is working for you. Yes, you will give the massage when the person schedules, but they are very spread out and some are never redeemed. I found a pattern with online gift certificate sales where I knew to expect money during certain times of the year. Christmas was the biggest with Valentine's Day second.

Where to Place your Gift Certificate Button

As we discussed in "Navigation," clear and simple is the key. Make your "Gift Certificate" button very easy to find and place it in more than one place one your website. I mean OBVIOUS to find. It should be on your home page of course. I like to place it in the header and footer so no matter which page the customer is on, they will see it.

Look at the space in this header **above** the "Schedule Appointment" button. My Gift Certificate button was there. It had the same shape as schedule appointment but it was **orange.** I wanted it to stand out and scream "click me!" to visitors. It was out of the ordinary coloring compared to the rest of my website and it was OBVIOUS. It wasn't neon orange, but it flowed nicely with the muted colors and still stood out. Putting the button in the header allowed it to show up on every page. I also put the button in the footer of every page. This was beneficial because after a visitor scrolled down reading a page, they would see the gift certificate button again. They wouldn't need to scroll back to the top to click.

Above is the footer which was placed on every page of the website. The **orange "Gift Certificate" button was below the "Schedule Appointment" button.** But wait, I put more links in my website to buy gift certificates. I placed it in the secondary menu under "Home."

There was also a clickable link on the services page. Overkill maybe, but the more times you put something in front of your customer, the better chances they remember you when they want a gift certificate if they aren't looking for it right then.

You will want to add your policy on redeeming gift certificates somewhere. Possibly write a sentence or two on the landing

76

page where they make the purchase. Also, each gift certificate has a place to print your policy directly on it, so whoever receives the gift knows your businesses policies. In my state, Gift Certificates can't expire, so we use verbiage like: "Gift Certificates do not expire. They are transferable but may not be exchanged for cash."

We also didn't allow refunds but made every effort to use the dollar amount for something else like product.

I really encouraged them to give it to someone else if they weren't going to use it. We always liked new client's coming in the door.

People love quick and easy. They want instant and some procrastinators need instant. Selling gift certificates from your website is easy for you and easy for the customer. It's a win-win!

ACTIVITY: Does your business intend to sell gift certificates? What aspect of your business could be sold as a gift certificate? Almost all businesses can call something a gift. Decide if you will sell gift certificates online and in store or just online. Decide on the best places to list your gift certificate button around your website. Happy Sales!

Notes and Research

CHAPTER EIGHT CHECKLIST

☐ Complete the activity for this chapter.

☐ If you want to sell online gift certificates, do a Google search for "sell gift cards from my website." Find a company you like and sign-up for a trial.

☐ Decide where on your website to place your "Gift Certificate" button. It should be very obvious and in multiple locations. Make it big and bright if your business lends itself to gifting.

☐ Online gift certificates are good customer service and once set up, don't require anything from you! It's all automated, from the client paying, then receiving the gift certificate, to you getting the money. Plus, you get new customers!

☐ Look up the fee per transaction with the company you decide to use. Consider adding a "convenience fee" at checkout so you don't lose money with each online sale.

Chapter 9
Online Scheduling

Scheduling appointments can be very time consuming and often a hassle. Whether the customer doesn't have their calendar in front of them or they are really indecisive about where to add you to their already overflowing schedule, scheduling some people takes LOTS of time. You wait for them to think and start to say yes, then remember they had a dentist appointment at that time and you offer a new time, but they can't do that. They pick a day and it's the only day you aren't in the office. Then they look through their phone calendar for a while, as you offer another time, and they say they think it should work. As a business owner, you don't want to hear "I think that should work." To me that doesn't sound like a committed appointment.

While running your business, you will wear many hats, and anytime you can remove a task from your list of duties, take advantage of it. Having a scheduling calendar online gives the customer the freedom to see your availability at a glance and take as long as they need to pick the best time for them. And it's available 24/7.

> The time saving advantages to having an online scheduling system is worth far more than the $20 a month cost.

I don't know how many times I had clients say they loved scheduling online because they could do it when it crossed their mind at 10:30 at night.

Another big time-saving advantage to having an online scheduler on your website is you eliminate tasks like making reminder phone calls, rescheduling when something comes up and they need to move their appointment, or playing phone tag to schedule in the first place. Everyone leads busy lives, and a key tool to making your business run smoothly in the 21st Century is having an online schedule. Everyone from hairstylists to attorneys can use an appointment scheduler. If you remodel kitchens, there needs to be an appointment for you to see and bid the project. If you sell clothing in a boutique, there needs to be an appointment for your personal shopper service. If you make cakes, there needs to be an appointment to meet with the bride-to-be for sampling. If you offer pet sitting, there needs to be an appointment for you to meet the pets and get feeding instructions. If you own a coffee shop or grocery store, you need an appointment to arrange curbside pickup. Almost every business can use an online scheduler to make appointments for something.

Online Scheduler Features

You're in control of your schedule. During set up, you put in your availability for appointments, and that is all the customer gets to see. If it's not an option, they can't pick it. This avoids overbooking or double-booking. When someone picks a time, you get an email with the choice to accept, decline, or reschedule. This gives you a double-checking system in case something came up and the spot is no longer available. You do have the option to turn the accept/decline feature off if you would rather one less step and automatically give the customer their choice. You will get an email that you have a new appointment which has already been added to your calendar. It's a beautiful thing!

Safety for self-employed, service-based providers

A word about online scheduling when you work alone. The beauty of having your business online is you can reach so many people. With that brings lots of strangers. Aunt Jenny isn't referring all your clients anymore. In the massage industry, there is a need to weed out the "creepers." Those customers who are looking for something more sexual in nature is an unfortunate reality in the massage scheduling world.

Any self-employed business owner who is meeting a customer for the first time while alone in the office should take note of the following safety tip.

Talk over the phone before the customer comes to their first appointment. If the customer already booked an appointment online, give them a call to find out more in depth what they are needing. You can tell over the phone if the person is "not your kind of client" and be clear about what your business does and does not do.

This phone call is a good time to tell the customer about your cancelation policies and any helpful tips for finding your office or where to park. You get to feel them out and they get to ask any questions they may have.

I never see a new client for the first time without having a verbal conversation with them prior to their first visit.

Some online scheduling systems have a feature where a new client can't book an appointment without calling first. This may be a deterrent to some customers, but if they really want to get an appointment with you, they will call.

Automated email or text reminders

You will have the option to set the length of time the reminder goes out before the scheduled appointment. I had a 24-hour cancellation policy, so my reminder when out 48 hours before their appointment. Most people appreciate the reminder and it will reduce no shows or miscommunication about the day or time they were scheduled.

Automated emails

Another value-added feature of the scheduler I used was automatic email templates. I had one template set to email clients who hadn't been in for an appointment for 3 months. It was a friendly reminder that it was time to schedule a massage and let them know we were thinking about them. Another automatic email went out to clients on their birthday and wished them a special day. People loved those, and they brought back business. You can create a template email for any occasion and customize it yourself or use a pre-written one on the software.

This alone is worth $20 a month! If you like the idea of this feature, make sure the scheduler you pick offers it.

Customers can make an account

When your customer makes an account, all previous and upcoming appointments are recorded on their account page. At a glance they can see when they were last in and what service they received as well as when their next appointment is.

Customers can reschedule at their convenience

This is convenient for everyone. They can instantly change their appointment to another day or time and even leave you a note as to why if they want. You get an email about the change and it's done! Easy and efficient.

It keeps track of your metrics

Most schedulers will have options to run reports for things like which service is most often completed or showing the number of 60-minute massages versus 90-minute massages in a given time frame. It shows how people scheduled, online or not, and how many services each employee performed. Having this insight helps you identify business trends, strengths and weaknesses.

Keeping track of sales

Many online schedulers will track your sales and sync to your bookkeeping software if you choose. Plus, customers can pay online BEFORE their appointment if you choose to offer that.

There are many online scheduling calendars available for you to choose. Within your industry, you may find one better suited than another based on your business's needs. I suggest doing a search online or seeing what other people in your line of business are using. There will be a monthly fee starting around $20 and up with many companies offering a free trial period. There are multiple options and features available as the price gets higher. To start, you may only need the basics, so begin low in cost, and if you need more features in the future you can upgrade at that time.

The scheduler will walk you through how to add the "book now" button to your website. You will be able to customize the look of your button slightly. It really doesn't take much time, and you have tech support available to you when you need it. Remember, your website builder tech support can help you with anything about your website. It's exciting to add this feature and have appointments booked while you sleep!

The picture above is how my "Schedule Appointment" button looked on my website. It was also placed on the footer of every page and under each service description there was a "book now" button which took the customer to the scheduling page.

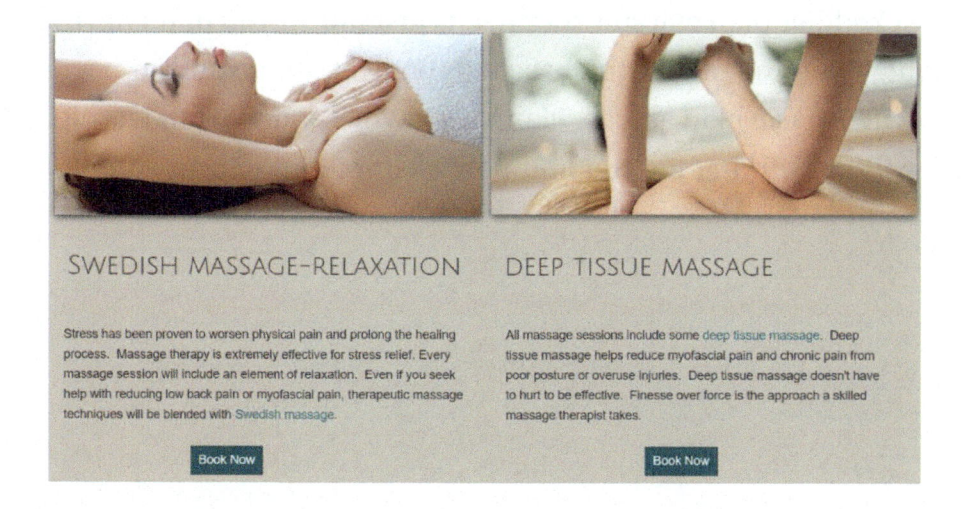

SWEDISH MASSAGE-RELAXATION

Stress has been proven to worsen physical pain and prolong the healing process. Massage therapy is extremely effective for stress relief. Every massage session will include an element of relaxation. Even if you seek help with reducing low back pain or myofascial pain, therapeutic massage techniques will be blended with Swedish massage.

Book Now

DEEP TISSUE MASSAGE

All massage sessions include some deep tissue massage. Deep tissue massage helps reduce myofascial pain and chronic pain from poor posture or overuse injuries. Deep tissue massage doesn't have to hurt to be effective. Finesse over force is the approach a skilled massage therapist takes.

Book Now

ACTIVITY: Decide which part of your business could be scheduled online, giving the customer the liberty to do it on their own and freeing up your time for other things. If your main product isn't a service, maybe a lower scheduler plan will suit your needs just fine. If you don't have a high volume of customers scheduling yet, then you can begin with a basic plan as well. Plan for growth, though. Your website will be working for you and new customers will find you and want to schedule.

Notes and Research

CHAPTER NINE CHECKLIST

☐ Complete the activity for this chapter.

☐ Find an online scheduling product that works for your business needs. This will be a time saver if it suits your business.

☐ Look at the features that come with your online scheduler. You may find the metrics tracker or the sales uploading to your bookkeeping software really helpful and worth choosing one company over another.

☐ Set up the "schedule now" button front and center on your home page as well as on all other pages of your website. The header and footer are good places to easily repeat the button on every page.

☐ Think about new-client processes for booking appointments to eliminate any "creepers" and maintain your safety while working alone. Many sole proprietor businesses see clients one on one with no other people in the office. Make that phone call to them before their first appointment or decide what your policies will be.

☐ Once set-up, test the "schedule now" button to make sure the process is smooth for your customers and everything is working.

Congratulations! This is a good time to publish your website if you haven't already done so. Go ahead and make it live so the public can see it. You will still be making changes and modifications but you've got all the important pieces done!

WAY TO GO!

Chapter 10
Social Media

We all know and use social media, and you may already understand why it's good for your business. Social media lets your customers get to know you and interact with you even when they are away from your office. Some people spend many hours of their day on social media, and seeing your business should be part of what comes across their screen. Social media can be used for giving a behind-the-scenes look at the daily operations of your business, introducing a new product or staff member, telling people about a special you're running or a product you're offering. The uses for social media are only limited by your imagination. Some days it may just be a simple post with an uplifting phrase or picture. It's a great way to show the personality of your business, build your brand and build rapport with your customers. It's fun to see customers' comments and responses to your posts and it keeps your business fresh in their mind so they think of you when they need your service.

Types of Social Media

There are many options for social media. Facebook, Instagram, Twitter, LinkedIn, Pinterest, and YouTube are a few. Let's cover the basics and how you may use them to your benefit. You probably aren't going to need all of these platforms, and some will be more useful to you depending on your type of business.

Facebook

You may already have a Facebook account for yourself personally, but you will need to create one with your business name. If you don't already have a personal profile, Facebook will want you to make one before you can add a business page. The business page has a nice platform that not only can be integrated to your website but can be linked to your online scheduling software too. You can list your services, prices, add some pictures, office hours, and address to make your business FB page complete. It's like a mini website with the ability to post real time happenings.

Some ways you can use Facebook for your business are listing upcoming events your business is hosting or creating a live class to teach something to your customers. People can like your page, share it with friends, and leave you reviews. This is the beauty of social media. Your customers can help build your business. You can even go live on Facebook if you are at an event or want to make a video about something you're promoting.

Again, here your options are endless and if you like to be in front of the camera. People love watching videos. If you don't have time for videos or don't want to be on camera, you can post about anything to promote your business. Look around at other businesses to get ideas. You may already be a Facebook pro, so this one can be easy and fun. Posting 3 times a week is minimum, and every day is ideal for Facebook.

> The uses for social media are only limited by your imagination! Find a platform you enjoy and get started.

Instagram

Instagram is a platform for pictures and videos. You can show photos of your business or services or products. Your goal should be to get your customers to follow you on Instagram, so when they look at their account, your business's posts will be right there. Like Facebook, it's another way to remind them you are there and keep information coming through pictures with captions and hashtags about your topic.

For example, if a clothing boutique gets new shipments on Tuesdays, they could get in the routine of unpacking, putting on display and picturing the post on Instagram. Captions could include what colors the item comes in and how it fits or what to pair it with for a complete look. If you are a hair stylist you can show before and after pictures. Skincare professionals may like to share a short video of a partial facial or applying a face mask. You get the idea. There is some room here to show things about your personal life. People like to connect with you on a human level, but don't stray too far from your business focus.

Sign up for a business account and get posting with these clear strategies in mind. Know who you're trying to reach. Decide what you would like to accomplish by using Instagram. You may have goals to gain likes, follows, and comments while you're becoming known, but ultimately, you'd like to convert sales. Decide and stick with your posting schedule. Once you have followers, they will expect you to post, and they'll be looking for it.

It is suggested to post once or twice a day. Hashtags help make your content searchable. When someone searches for a hashtag, they will see all related content, yours included. This is a way to get new views and followers. The more you get involved and comment on other Instagram pages, the more you will be recognized. Like all social media, the more you put into it, the more you get out of it.

> Social media needs some consistency to be successful. Decide on a posting schedule and stick with it.

Twitter

Twitter is a social media platform known for short (140 characters at a time) messages known as Tweets. You will create a bio for your Twitter account where you are limited to 160 characters. Get creative and get your message across short and sweet. Explain what you do and the benefit of using your service or product. Add your logo for your profile picture. Once your bio is set up, you can begin to click around the Twitter platform. Search keywords related to what you do and see what conversations are going on. If you can add value to one of them, chime in, but don't automatically try to plug your business. I like this rule for all social media. Provide value first and the sales naturally will follow. Once you have a rapport with customers, what you say carries more weight. You can post facts, links, or quotes, and people will like and retweet them. Keep tweets relevant to your company because those people are following you for that reason. Tweeting 10-50 times per day is normal. Yes, this is a lot, but remember, you don't have to use this social media platform. Decide if Twitter is one you would like to try or not.

Pinterest

This is mainly a site where your pictures will draw your followers. I don't find it as useful for a service like massage, but I've had some creative colleagues make it work for them. Pinterest is great for sharing recipes, home ideas, style inspiration, and other ideas to try. Pinterest users look for their hobbies or ideas about something they want to try. For example, a business may create and post pictures of nails, hair, or makeup ideas, and when a customer likes what they see, they "pin it" to their personal board. These posts by the business should always have a way to bring the customer back to their website, added to their mailing list, or get more information to purchase something. They are customer prospects, and you want to turn them into long-term customers. The more pictures posted, the more chance your business has of being found.

An ideal use of Pinterest for a company would go like this: Suzie is remodeling her bathroom. She wants to hang a barn door at the entrance. Suzie goes to Pinterest for ideas on what type of barn door. She falls in love with one and clicks on the picture. It takes her to the website where she can pick the size and color and have her questions answered. She orders the door. Success! That is what every company's goal should be. Get the sale from the picture posted. Be creative and use Pinterest if it suits your business.

LinkedIn

This platform is a place to network and to hire someone or put an ad out that you're looking to hire. As your business gets started, you may want to use LinkedIn as a professional network to introduce yourself and your company and find others you know who are already there. It seems like every profession uses LinkedIn. You can find others in your industry or connect with like-minded industries. While you grow your professional network, you may also generate new business leads and nurture referral sources. Your business page can tell your story, engage with people, and share career opportunities while you become a trusted source. Like other social media, posting engaging content makes people follow you. You can introduce new products or services or post discounts or special offers. Differentiate yourself from competitors and share what makes you unique. LinkedIn is another way for your company to show up in search engines, so always have links to your website in posts.

YouTube

Everyone's watched a YouTube video for something. Even if it's a "how to" or a cooking recipe, videos are fun and easy to watch. Once you have a YouTube channel for your business, it's another place Google finds you on the web. You could share your knowledge about your business through YouTube videos. Here are some examples for the massage therapy industry. Make a video of how you do a certain hand massage technique. Use video for after-session client homework if they forgot how to do the hip stretch you assigned them. Add other how-to stretch videos to the YouTube channel. Make a video demonstrating at-home exercises for people suffering from frozen shoulders. Use email to send clients the direct links to which videos are most appropriate for them. It's your own library of resources and is great customer service. Plus, it increases the likelihood the clients will do their homework in between sessions.

> Retweeted, pinned, liked, and followed are all good things!

Are you still thinking, "I wouldn't know what to make a video about"? It's as easy as thinking about common questions you get asked about what you do. Maybe it's how you get the frosting to look so perfect on your cakes or your technique in potty training a puppy. Maybe you can share the way you put a complete outfit together out of someone's clothes they already own, or how to repurpose a wooden pallet into a piece of furniture. These videos are easily taken from your cell phone and uploaded onto your YouTube channel. You will want to put keywords everywhere in your video description to increase chances of being found by strangers who are searching the web.

There isn't a set number of videos you need to upload to your channel nor a frequency. You can relax more with YouTube and make new videos when you think of them. I will advise making a social media schedule, though. If you never make a goal for how often you add to your YouTube channel, months will go by without any new content. YouTube videos can be any length, so you aren't as limited with short videos like on some other sites.

> Social media is free to use, so jump in and get your feet wet. Remember, how much you put in will be how much you get out of it.

Social media is free to use so why not take advantage of another source of marketing? I have often lamented to fellow business owners maintaining my social media alone is a full-time job. You can hire a company to do this for you, but in the beginning when funds are tight, set it up yourself and start slow.

You may love this part of marketing for your business or, if you're like me, it is a necessary evil. Remember, you can trade services or find a college student to do your social media accounts for you. I used college students who needed internship hours in a medical clinic (usually pre-physical therapy majors) to add to their resumes. The students had many other tasks, but social media came naturally to them, and many liked it. Yes, you still need to give direction as it is your company. So, make suggestions on a topic or idea and let them run with it. Make sure you approve the posts before they go live.

Set a schedule for your social media. As with your bookkeeping, re-ordering inventory, rescheduling clients, and all the other day-to-day tasks you have when running your business, updating your social media needs to be on your schedule. Whichever platforms you decide to use–remember, you don't have to use all of these–write down when you are posting each week. Maybe Mondays/Wednesday/Friday is Facebook, daily at 2:00PM is Instagram, and every other week is a new YouTube video. You will find what works for you, but write it down. There are ways you can pre-enter your posts, and schedule them to go out when you choose, so if you would rather get all social media done for the week on Monday morning, then that option may appeal to you.

ACTIVITY: Look into the social media platforms you aren't familiar with and see if they may be useful for your business. Ask a friend or family member who uses one to help you understand the basics, or do what I like to do and jump in and start clicking around. Observe what's happening around the platform, and see if you're drawn to it. You may also keep it simple and begin with getting your business on one or two of the platforms you already use. Pick one and take action. You're doing this to build your online profile and have those ideal customers find you. Look at the big picture and your future success. It's worth it!

Notes and Research

CHAPTER TEN CHECKLIST

☐ Complete the activity for this chapter.

☐ Which social media platform do you like the best or where are your ideal clients/customers hanging out? If you have a decorating company and know your customers are on Pinterest, that's where you should be too.

☐ Set a schedule for social media and stick to it. Being consistent once a week is better than posting in spurts.

☐ Link your social account to your website, and vice versa. It could be the Facebook logo in your footer for example so when customers click on it, they are taken over to your Facebook page. Conversely, Facebook can send them to your website with a click.

☐ Start with one social media platform and once you have it mastered, add another one. The more places your business has a presence, the more listings it will have on Google. This helps new customers find you.

Chapter 11
Blog

A blog is an informational website or web page of sorts. It is regularly updated and often written in an informal or conversational way. Some people think of their blog posts like a diary and put into words what is happening or what they are feeling at that time. Sometimes a blog can be used for discussion or as a place to voice your views on certain topics. Blogs are displayed in reverse chronological order so the most recent post is at the top of the page. The difference between your website and your blog is mainly the fact that your blog will contain frequently updated content where your website is mainly static and organized into pages. Your blog can be linked and shown on your website, which I would suggest, but it could also stand alone. Some people even use their blog as their website.

> You don't have to be a great writer to start your own blog. You can even dictate your blog post if typing isn't your strength.

As long as you have a passion for your topic, you can write conversationally and put information into words. You started a business, so you must be passionate about what you do. Tell people what you do, how you do it, stories about when you were successful or not, and give examples of things people can do from home. Your blog will be focused around your business type but will include things like current events, pictures, and infographics. A good blog post will be 400-1000 words, quick and easy to read, and say something interesting or useful.

If we use a cake baker as an example, their passion is baking beautiful, delicious, and sometimes unique cakes to sell to the public. Their blog may talk to the people who want to buy their cakes as well as the at-home bakers who want to learn how to make a better cake. The blog can have posts about how to bake different types of cakes. During various times of the year, there could be posts about seasonal cakes and recipes to try. There might be blog posts about making your own cream cheese frosting with tips for success. A post could share about when an ingredient was substituted, and the result was less than desired. If there is a local charity the bakery wants to support or an event happening, the blog can talk about those. Posts can include current events. Maybe they want to organize a "Bake and Take" for charity day where the public comes and bakes a cake to take home, and the proceeds goes to a charity. You get the idea. A blog can cover a wide variety of topics, but don't leave your business's main focus too far behind as you explore post topics.

There is an art to blogging for SEO, Search Engine Optimization, which is why there are companies you can pay to blog and optimize your posts for you. I found all the SEO too overwhelming to learn thoroughly and I never would have started blogging if I had waited to learn it first. We will explain SEO in a later chapter because it is applicable to many of the chapters in this book. My advice is to just begin. Take one blog at a time and write when inspiration hits. Get inspiration from other social media sources, your daily life, and things that are happening in your community.

If you aren't good at typing, there are apps and software where you can dictate your post, and it will type for you. You still need to edit, but it may save you time. Some people communicate better by speaking than by writing. Find what works for you and write without thinking. You can go back and edit before you publish and can always edit the post if you find a mistake after publishing, so just get the words on paper. Let your personality show, and add pictures and glimpses into your life so people connect with you.

Blogging daily isn't necessary. One to two blogs per week is enough and allows you to get solid ideas and content ready to make a good post. If it feels like a chore, reduce the number you're doing. For some it works to pre-plan topics so if you're rushed to post one week the content doesn't come out subpar. Also remember to link your blog back to your website. If there is more information on your website, you can make a certain phrase in your blog clickable to take the reader over to your website to read further. Or ask visitors to subscribe to your mailing list and link to your website.

Blogging is free and can be set up through multiple different companies. Word Press and Google's Blogger are two options. The website builder you use when making your website may have a blog option included. I include a blog as one of the more essential pieces for your business. Link your blog to your website and with each blog post. Your website gets a refreshing boost of content which makes search engines favor your site.

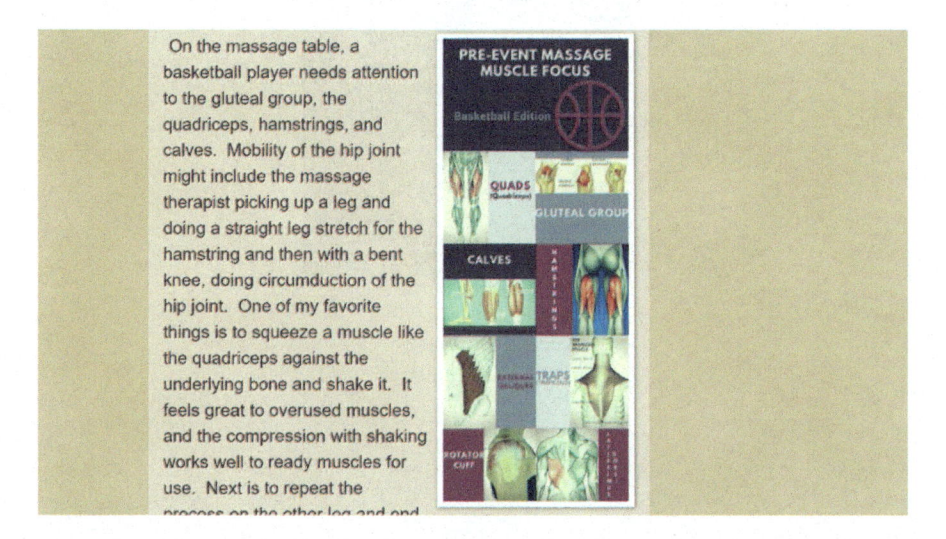

The example above is an excerpt from one of my blog posts about sports massage. The picture displaying information about which muscles need attention for a basketball player is called an infographic or pictograph. These are a popular way to provide information. You can create your own with fun apps like Canva.

The example below shows a pictograph which pulls key points from the blog post and displays them separately so at a glance the reader can get the idea of the post. You will include your logo and a call to action at the bottom of each blog post.

The most significant symptom of these conditions is pain. Pain centered around the hips and shoulders, along with headaches is a huge indicator of the conditions. Other symptoms include unexplained fever, cough, and sore throat, swelling, jaw pain, trouble getting up in the morning, weight loss, and depression. Another huge sign for massage therapists is if the client is not responding well to massage and either gets worse or stays the same for a long period of time. If you are experiencing a combination of these symptoms, please consult your doctor before continuing massage.

The good news about PMR and GCA is that they are both easily treatable by steroid anti-inflammatory medication. Massage is a great way to complement the treatment once some relief has been seen in the patient. Massage is not recommended without the approval of a physician first when a client is suffering from PMR and GCA.

Diagnostic Criteria for PMR and GCA

- Over the age of 50 ✓
- Pain for more than a month in the shoulder, neck, or pelvic girdle. ✓
- One hour or more of morning stiffness ✓
- New or abnormal headache, scalp pain, or neck pain ✓

MASSAGE LA MESA

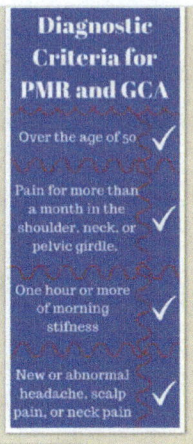

ACTIVITY: Do you follow a blogger already? What is it about their style that keeps you coming back to read their next post? Even if you don't follow a blogger, you most likely have read a blog before. When you search the internet for answers to a topic, the results are bound to show a blog or two. If you are naturally blessed with humor in your nature, let it show in your writing. Quirky and fun intertwined with great content will bring readers to your blog in no time!

Notes and Research

CHAPTER ELEVEN CHECKLIST

☐ Complete the activity for this chapter.

☐ Consider starting a blog and putting it on your website. This is a good way to keep fresh content on your website which will bring more people to you.

☐ Your website builder may have a blog you can use. If not, search online for free blogs. Google's "Blogger" is an easy one to get started with.

☐ Even if you don't like to type, you can find dictation services that will turn what you say into a blog post in no time. You'll still need to read it and make edits, but it might be the preferred method for some business owners.

☐ Remember, the blog is free to start and maintain. It's a time investment rather than a money investment. It will be an additional way Google will bring new customers to your website. Not only that, it's good information about your product or service. The reader will see you as the expert and think of you when they need your service.

Chapter 12

Content is King – Beyond the basics

There is a saying in the SEO world, "Content is King." If there is any one how-to-get-found-online tip to stand the test of time, this would be it. Continually adding quality content to your website, blog, and social media will bring you returns with the search engines.

You already have basic content pages for your website. You have the home page, services, prices, about, and contact pages. Let's look at examples of other pages you can add to your website to help with content.

Intake Forms

For me being in a service industry such as massage, I have paperwork each client needs to fill out before their first appointment. I found it is good customer service to have those forms available on my website if someone wanted to fill them out prior to their appointment.

FAQs

I had many people who were new to massage ask the same questions about their first session so I wrote "What to Expect" and gave it a page on my website. It explained before, during, and after information to make the first timer feel as comfortable as possible.

> If there is one SEO tip that has stood the test of time, "Content Is King" is it.

Links

There is a belief in SEO that links to your website and links from your website rank you higher with internet searches. Especially important are the links from other websites to yours or outside links. The links need to be quality. You should personally know these other people or businesses who are linking to your website. I had a page on my website which listed and linked to other businesses I found complementary to my own business and helpful for clients who used massage as part of their wellness routine. For example, a chiropractor, acupuncturist, a personal trainer, or yoga instructor might do this or a physical therapy clinic or a sports medicine practice. Since you know these people personally, they usually will link their website to yours in return.

It's similar to a "Recommended Professionals" page. It's like a word-of-mouth referral. Think about other businesses that complement yours and reach out to the ones you believe would benefit your business.

Another outside link idea is writing articles for other websites. Before I started a blog, I wrote informational articles and put them each on a page of my website. These covered topics I got the most questions about or the most common ailments I saw in clients. This easily became ideas for blog posts, but they remained on my website as content. I found a website called Ezine articles where I could post the articles about massage in the health and wellness category. Each article contained a link to my website (external link) and the most-read articles showed up on search engine listings when my business was searched online. The search engines value websites with more external links. They place them higher on search results, and the more traffic an external link has, the more valuable it is for your website. For example, if Ezine's website has 600,000 visitors each month, Google says they are more popular (worth noticing) than my business with 600 visitors. Therefore, if my business has links coming from a popular, high-traffic site than in Google's eyes, maybe my website is worth noticing, too. When my website is worth noticing, it shows up higher in search results. Find other websites you can use to link to yours. Maybe there is a website displaying cake recipes where you could post recipes or a fitness website that your business fits for the sale of your water bottles. Do a little bit of research to see if you can find external link sources for your website.

Resources

I used this page for client homework info, mostly. Our clinic always gave homework for the client to get the most out of their massage session, and so they knew we were in a partnership to help achieve their goals. At minimum, there were stretches they needed to do at home. The resources page contained links to the stretches, how to do them, and how long to hold them. Even though each client was walked through how to do the stretch in the office, they usually forgot. Besides stretches, homework resources included how to foam roll a certain area, using a tennis ball for self-massage, and how to use the Thera-Cane for trigger points. You can have separate links for different videos on YouTube or separate pages with words and pictures to walk the client through. People love the feeling that you care enough to make sure they have the information to do it correctly which ultimately is showing you care their health improves.

Mission Statement

I believe there should be a section of your website that states your mission statement or purpose, beliefs, and goals about what you do. It gives a feel for the vision you have for your business and why you chose that business. Customers like to relate to this, and it helps them pick your business over another. Here is an example from a page on my website.

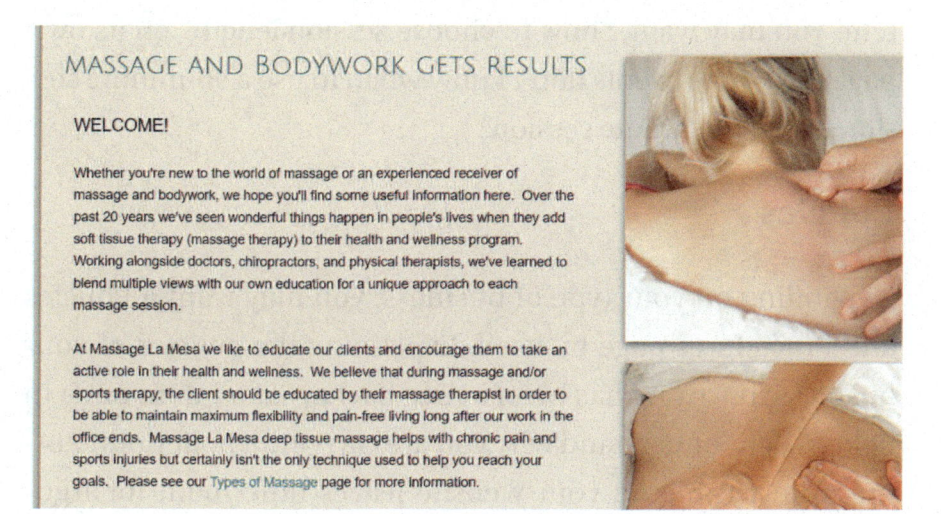

MASSAGE AND BODYWORK GETS RESULTS

WELCOME!

Whether you're new to the world of massage or an experienced receiver of massage and bodywork, we hope you'll find some useful information here. Over the past 20 years we've seen wonderful things happen in people's lives when they add soft tissue therapy (massage therapy) to their health and wellness program. Working alongside doctors, chiropractors, and physical therapists, we've learned to blend multiple views with our own education for a unique approach to each massage session.

At Massage La Mesa we like to educate our clients and encourage them to take an active role in their health and wellness. We believe that during massage and/or sports therapy, the client should be educated by their massage therapist in order to be able to maintain maximum flexibility and pain-free living long after our work in the office ends. Massage La Mesa deep tissue massage helps with chronic pain and sports injuries but certainly isn't the only technique used to help you reach your goals. Please see our Types of Massage page for more information.

Services

You already made a services page for your basic website navigation. You can and probably need to elaborate a bit on each service. For my business customers, they needed to be educated about deep tissue massage and that it didn't have to hurt to be effective. I put that on a page. People also had many misconceptions about receiving massage during pregnancy. There was one page of information about prenatal massage and its safety and another page of frequently asked questions. We used neuromuscular therapy (trigger point therapy) as a technique often in the office and found the general public didn't know what that was, so it went on a page. You can write a page to explain each service more in depth. This benefits you because you're adding more content to your website and only the people who are interested in reading further on a topic have to click on it to go to the next page. So, if you offer 5 services and you have the basic service page with links to five other pages, you just increased your content! You may want, "how to choose session length" on its own page too. Some clients don't know when to use a 90-minute session over a 60-minute session.

Policies

Depending on your type of business, you may want a Policies and Procedures page by itself. Explaining the policies of your business in writing has been a nice backup more than once to help a client understand why you are carrying a policy out. Putting it in writing on your website leaves little room for argument.

All of these ideas can be adjusted to fit your business. I hope my examples trigger ideas for pages for your own website to build content. As time passes and you think of things pertaining to your business, add a page about it. It can't hurt. Massage La Mesa's website had 37 pages of what I would like to believe was quality content. I began with 5 pages, and I know my website performed well, successfully bringing in many new clients each month, so I'm a believer that content is king. I also believe **there is no one thing that makes your business successful online. You will need the perfect blend of many of these ideas**.

You being an entrepreneur and starting your own business is enough to make me believe you have it in you to get this done. Find what drives you and give it your all. Every page of your website, every post on your social media, and every blog written gets you closer to your goals. Every day you work on your business brings you closer to the success you deserve.

ACTIVITY: Brainstorm possibilities of additional content pages for your website. Make a list of every little part of what you do. What seems second nature to you isn't to most of the public. You are an expert in your area of business. The terminology or tools specific to your business that you use daily aren't things the public knows about. You can write about these. If it seems trivial to you, remember you went through a lot of training and time and experience before it became common place for you. Put yourself in a beginner's mind set and educate your potential customers with this information added to your website.

Notes and Research

CHAPTER TWELVE CHECKLIST

☐ Complete the activity for this chapter.

☐ Brainstorm ideas for other pages you can create for your website. Examples from this chapter are intake forms or paperwork that first-time clients need to fill out, a frequently asked questions page, a what to expect during your first appointment page, and a resources page where you recommend complementary items or other businesses.

☐ If content is king, then adding more and more pages to your website is a smart investment in your business. Google will like your website more and more. Start a planner with the dates you will publish new pages to your website.

☐ Is there a question about a part of your business you answer all the time? This is a good topic to write about on a designated page on your website.

☐ Work on getting links (inbound) to your website from other websites and link your website (outbound) to other websites when you have permission.

Chapter 13
SEO – Search Engine Optimization

If you aren't already familiar with the acronym SEO, now you'll begin to notice it all over the place. Search Engine Optimization is talked about everywhere, and it's imperative you have an understanding of how it effects your website. I think the reason it's always a hot topic is no one really knows how it works exactly and the rules (algorithms) keep changing.

In a nutshell, SEO is optimizing your website to be found as search engines crawl or scan the internet for information. When a user types something into the search bar, search engines crawl all information around the internet to bring the most relevant content to the searcher.

When you have good SEO, your keywords help your website to show up on results for your area of business. Your blog and social media are also a place where SEO matters. Your goal is to show up at the top of the results page on a search relating to your business.

Think of when you've used the internet to find something in the past. How many times have you gone to the second page of results? Never, I bet. Most users are the same, and if your company shows up on the second page of search results, don't expect to get a lot of phone calls. So, the challenge begins! How do you get to the top of results without paying for a company to help or paying for ads? We can talk about paid SEO later, but organic listings are where you want to spend your time.

Keywords

Your website builder will most likely have a SEO tool in it, and that's a good place to start. It will prompt you to add keywords on certain pages and in certain places. Your job is to know the most searched keywords in your industry and add those words to your website. Don't worry, there are keyword search tools available online for free to get you started. In my business of massage therapy, the most often searched keywords (at the time) where relaxation, deep tissue, and reflexology. So those were the words I included in multiple places throughout my website. This is very simplified because there are more keywords, of course, and you can use them all, but the beauty of knowing the main ones is they will bring you the greatest results.

If CBD oil is the new rage and I add a page about it to my website, then I will be found as the potential customer searches "CBD massage." The more content you have on your website, the more your site is logged by search engines in *multiple* keyword categories. So, the theory is you will show up more often near the top of the page when those categories or keywords are searched. When I found the most searched keywords were relaxation, deep tissue, and reflexology, you better believe I wrote a page of content for each one.

The keyword research will also show if the competition for that word is high or low. This may be used to your advantage as becoming one of the first being found online for one aspect of what you do. For example, reflexology was highly searched, but there wasn't a lot of competition for it. I began to add reflexology content in different places in the hopes of it helping my SEO.

> The more content you have on your website, the more your site is logged by search engines in multiple keyword categories.

Google is by far the most widely used search engine. Yahoo and Bing round out the most popular after Google. If you need to choose keyword results from one of these search engines, use Google. Google is a monster, and isn't going anywhere anytime soon. The reason I mention this is for you to understand if you type "massage" into the search bar using Yahoo, you will get slightly different results than if you search "massage" using Google. Researching keywords for every search engine may be too time consuming, so start with Google.

Track Results

There are free tools to help you track your results. These are fun because you can see what people searched to land on your website. There is always power in knowledge and you can use the information to change keywords or SEO strategy as you see fit.

Alt tags, Meta tags, and Titles for your Web pages

As you build each page of your website, there is a *back end* of the site you will optimize for search engines. The *back end* is the part of your website the public doesn't see but the search engines do. Each of your web pages needs a title, and this title is noticed by the search engines above the content on the page. The better you title the page to its content using keywords, the more accurately the search engines categorize your page. There are also Meta tags and Alt tags on each page of your website. Both of these areas will need keywords added to help you show up on results. The website builder you use will prompt you to add these tags and titles to your web pages.

Multiple Domain Names

When we discussed picking your domain name and naming your business, SEO had a hand in the way we did that.

PRO TIP:

I had more than one professional marketer comment my business name Massage La Mesa was brilliant for SEO. It lends itself nicely to organic listings because of the way people search what they are looking for. They want a massage and they live in La Mesa. Another popular search is "massage near me," which my business would also pop up for because

Google knows the location you're searching from. I bought additional domain names to help with search engines finding my business. Massage91942.com, Massage91941.com, SportsMassageLaMesa.com, LaMesaMassageTherapy.com, and PrenatalMassageLaMesa.com. By using the zip codes around my office and the types of massage clients I wanted to attract, I gave myself a better chance to be listed on search results. I didn't make a separate website for all of these domains, but pointed them to my main website MassageLaMesa.com. With each domain name costing $10 a year (at the time), I figured $50 was worth the added help to my organic listing.

> Organic search engine listings are hard to get but worth the effort.

External Links

There is proof that search engines see you as more popular or worthy of ranking high on results if you have links from high traffic sites coming into your website. Links are when an outside source, say the Chamber of Commerce in your area, links from their website to yours. It doesn't have to be your website; it could be linking to your blog or social media. Maybe you sponsored a local event, and your business is mentioned in the city's email newsletter with a link to your website and then another link to your blog article about the event. Links going **to and from** your website make search engines take notice. Your site must be important. The more links you can create for yourself the better.

SEO is one of those areas you can easily find conflicting advice. Some will say use keywords at the top of the page because Google gives more weight to those. Some will say using your keywords a handful of times on the page gets better results.

The bottom line is no one really knows. If a company guarantees they can get you ranked #1 on Google, don't believe them and certainly don't pay them. My advice is to learn what you can using the free tools available, and then pay a professional when and if you're ready to move past the SEO basics. Ask around to find a referral you trust and often for a nominal fee they can help you to the next level or advise you how to make what you have better.

ACTIVITY: Search "keyword research tools" and start using a free tool to find the most used keywords in your area of business. Make a list of the top 50 keywords and look at that list every time you are ready to add a new page of content to your website. Look at the list when you create a blog post or post something on Facebook. Those keywords should always be handy and referred to often until you research the words again in 6 months.

Notes and Research

CHAPTER THIRTEEN CHECKLIST

- ☐ Complete the activity for this chapter.

- ☐ Do some Google basic keyword research for your business. You can simply type words related to your business into the Google search bar. For example, "cake frosting" has many other things pop up below it like cake frosting recipe, cake frosting tips, cake frosting tools, cake frosting ideas, and so on. These are possible keywords you can use.

- ☐ There are keyword research tools online you can use for free as well.

- ☐ The back end of the website is where you can add Alt tags, Meta tags and page titles using keywords. This will help your business be found online.

- ☐ Consider buying multiple domain names. Point the new domains to your main website.

- ☐ Get links to your website when you can.

Chapter 14
Review sites – Create an online reputation

When your business is new online, you want to gain customer reviews as quickly as possible. The online world is a beautiful extension of word-of-mouth referrals. Potential new customers will listen to what others are saying about you before they give you their business. The reviews help customers decide if your business is a good fit for what they need.

Whether you're providing a service or product, reviews are highly important to the success of your business. If you're like me, I always read reviews on Amazon and other shopping sites before I decide which product I buy. I do the same for restaurants, personal services, car repairs and pretty much everything. People will review the product or service itself, the customer service while getting that product and the experience as a whole. If they visit your place of business to get the product, they tend to review everything from how hard the location is to find, to parking, to their first impression while walking in the door and of course if they got what they expected. Visually they will make an immediate decision on appearance or cleanliness of the space and the first person they meet makes a huge difference on their overall thoughts about your business.

If you are a brick-and-mortar business, you have more work to do to earn those great reviews than those business who are online only. All businesses need to place customer service at the top of their list to be successful. You may have heard the term Customer Centric which many companies are using in training staff. I think it describes well what we are talking about. If you place the customer at the center of all your efforts, your business will succeed.

Where to Put Reviews to Gain the Biggest Impact for Your Business

There are many different sites online where customers can leave reviews. The ones I found help the most are Google, Yelp, and Facebook. There are also sites like TripAdvisor, Better Business Bureau (BBB) and Yellow Pages. Depending on your business type you decide which will benefit you the most.

Google

Google reviews are important and rank highly in results, especially if the customer is using Google as their search engine. When potential customers are searching online for a business like yours, the Google listing for your business will display and how many stars you have is front and center.

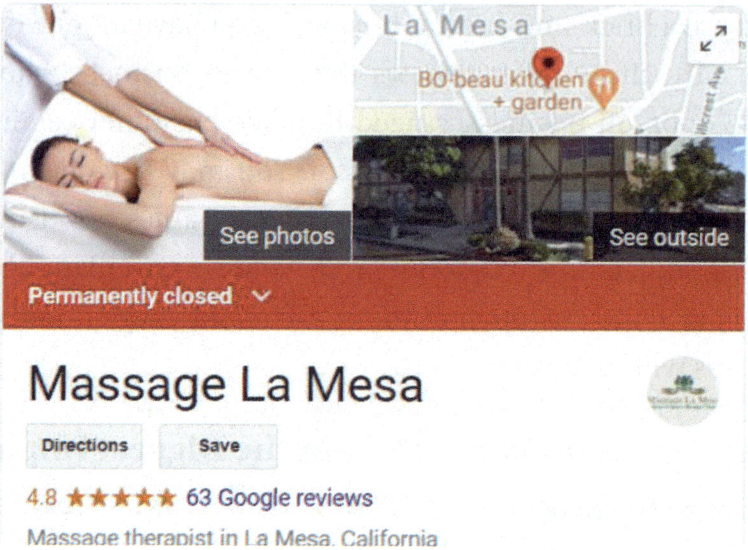
La Mesa
BO-beau kitchen + garden
See photos
See outside
Permanently closed
Massage La Mesa
Directions
Save
4.8 ★★★★★ 63 Google reviews
Massage therapist in La Mesa, California

By doing a quick search for anything in your area on Google you will see many examples of this. Below is a search result for "cakes" and you can see the Google maps listings that come up first with the name of the businesses and how many reviews they have.

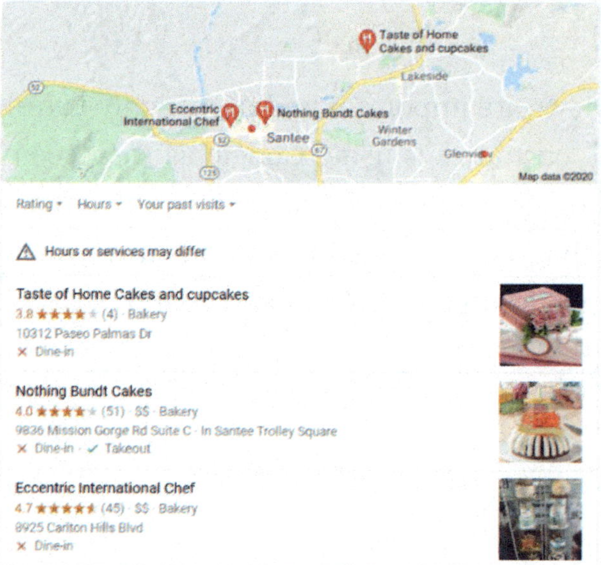
Taste of Home Cakes and cupcakes
Lakeside
Eccentric International Chef
Nothing Bundt Cakes
Santee
Winter Gardens
Map data ©2020
Rating · Hours · Your past visits
Hours or services may differ
Taste of Home Cakes and cupcakes
3.8 ★★★★★ (4) · Bakery
10312 Paseo Palmas Dr
Dine-in
Nothing Bundt Cakes
4.0 ★★★★★ (51) · $$ · Bakery
9836 Mission Gorge Rd Suite C · In Santee Trolley Square
Dine-in · Takeout
Eccentric International Chef
4.7 ★★★★★ (45) · $$ · Bakery
8925 Carlton Hills Blvd
Dine-in

You will need to add your business profile to Google so they have the correct information and then there is a place for customers to leave you those stellar reviews. *Google My Business* is where you customize your listing. Google is an easy platform for most customers to leave a review especially if they already have a Gmail address. This saves the step of creating an account.

Yelp

Yelp is really popular in my area on the west coast, USA. I've talked to business owners in other states who say they don't use it much. Wherever your business is located, you should know if people Yelp in your area. It is used so widely in my area that some businesses concentrate all of their marketing efforts to gain Yelp reviews alone. Yelp does things a little differently. They don't want you to solicit reviews. They have algorithms that crawl through the words used in reviews and they filter or remove reviews they think were "planted" or solicited. This is to preserve the authenticity of reviews. There are many guesses as to why some reviews get filtered and some don't. I have one theory which may contribute to some Yelp reviews being filtered. I believe if your review comes from a first time Yelper, it has a higher likelihood of being filtered. Another difference in Yelp reviews is not being able to remove a bad review. You may comment on the bad review, but it will always be there.

Yelp is easy and free to create a business profile. They have some nice features like messaging and appointment requests directly through their platform. Yelp is ranked very high on the results by Google, so it is worth making your company profile. In my experience, Yelp is used by the younger crowd, and I rarely had my 55+ clients leave Yelp reviews. If your business's demographics are the younger crowd, Yelp works well, and many are so used to Yelping, you don't have to ask for reviews.

Facebook

We discussed Facebook in the social media chapter, and because it's probably one of the social media platforms you will have for your business, it's easy to add reviews. Some say Facebook is becoming outdated, but it's still going strong for businesses, and I found it useful for marketing. With that in mind, ask a few customers or clients to leave your business a review to get you started.

As time goes by, others will leave reviews on their own, or you can spend one month asking people for Facebook reviews and the next month asking for Google reviews. As far as search engines go, Google holds more weight, but Facebook is good for friends to see what others say about your business. Each of these has their place, and you will decide which ones will benefit your business the most.

How to Get Reviews

If you find your business is open and you are serving customers but don't have any reviews yet, what do you do? Usually all you need to do is ask! Some people enjoy writing reviews, and they will review your company on their favorite platforms without any prompting. Those people are great, and we love them, but the majority of customers need to know you want them to review your business. By letting them know how much it helps your business grow, they are usually more than happy to write a review. This can be conveyed through a sign on the front desk or you asking them personally or an email explaining why you need their help with a link to the site where they can write their review.

Making it as easy as possible for the customer to successfully complete the review will increase your chances of people following through. I saw a business go as far as having a designated computer sitting on the front desk, so after checkout, you could write your review before you ever left the building. That's one way to make sure the person doesn't get busy and forget once they get home. If a customer returns to your business and compliments you about the product they bought, it's the perfect time to thank them and say, "Would you mind putting that in writing?"

> Reviews add credibility to your business and are an invaluable part of online marketing.

One challenge I ran into was the older population who wasn't as computer savvy and didn't want to create an account for the review sites. They thought they would get a bunch of unwanted emails and solicitations, plus not having reviewed businesses before, the whole thing was a headache for them. To make it as easy as possible, I made a step-by-step email to walk them through it. This increased the results a little, but you can't make anyone take the time to write a review.

You can offer small incentives like something added on to their service or a free giveaway. I wasn't a fan of discount offers, and realistically, they are either going to write a review as a favor to you or not. It does take time and energy to write your business a review, so be sure to send a big thank you to the ones who do!

Responding to Bad Reviews

Businesses are so scared of bad reviews. For good reason, too. These review sites have put the power into the hands of every consumer out there to use words against your business. Words which stay online and follow you forever. If you are offering the best customer service you can, then the bad reviews should be few and far between. You will get them, so being prepared when you do is the key to handling them with grace.

When you get a bad review, follow these helpful tips.

1. Take some time before you react with a written response.

2. Give people the benefit of the doubt.

3. Take the high road even if it's hard. Respond with a public answer apologizing for their disappointment and explain your side of the story briefly without putting blame on the customer. Stay general and professional in your response. You don't need to publicly say the reviewer is wrong and irrational (even if they are) or point out their faults in the events. Stick to the facts, and keep it professional.

The public is smart enough to know sometimes a business can't please everyone and people have bad days. One or two bad reviews don't break a business. Some say it makes them human. Obviously, many bad reviews will show a pattern and will make a potential customer think twice before giving that company their business. There is competition out there for every business type, so be the best you can be, and you won't need to worry about bad reviews sending customers elsewhere.

ACTIVITY: Begin by adding your business profile to Google My Business. Even if you're still working on your website, you can make a Google profile. Start asking customers to leave a review for your business and post a contest on social media asking for reviews in exchange for putting their name in a drawing to win a free "_____."

Notes and Research

CHAPTER FOURTEEN
CHECKLIST

☐ Complete the activity for this chapter.

☐ There are multiple places to get reviews on your business. Pick one or two to get started. Google is a good one. Set up a Google My business account.

☐ Some customers will leave reviews on their own, but most of the time, it helps to ask them to write a review about your business.

☐ Make a business profile on as many review sites as you can find. Although the focus of asking people to write a review will be directed to one or two sites, it doesn't hurt to have your profile up on additional sites.

☐ Answer any bad reviews promptly and professionally.

Chapter 15
How to get found online

Let's tie all this SEO, marketing, and website information together to make sure your business can be found online. After all, that's the purpose of your website. To get found online, your website needs to be optimized with keywords, Meta tags and plenty of content. Google is the beast of online search engines. Make Google as happy as you can, and your website will show at the top of searches. Here are my top 20 ways to get found online:

1. List your website profile on a Google business page.

2. Add social media sites, and your business will look more important to search engines.

3. Building an online reputation with social media and reviews will give customers the information they need to choose your business.

4. Write articles for professional publications or other professional sites where you gain a link to your website.

5. Get your business named online using a press release, Chamber of Commerce event, health fair, or farmer's market.

6. Donate a product or service to another business in exchange for mentioning your business in an email blast to their customers or link to your website.

7. Partner with a complementary business teaching a class or open house where each of you mention the other in marketing online for the event. Then get your local Chamber of Commerce to announce your event online.

8. Online algorithms are constantly changing, so keeping up with what's currently working is good practice. Spend time networking with other small business professionals in a group meeting or online meeting to share ideas and referrals.

9. Use keywords words for blogs and your website.

10. Get testimonials from clients who've used your service or product and share that online.

11. Make videos with keywords in the descriptions. It is thought that a video is 60% more likely to get ranked by search engines than a web page with the same content. Google likes videos.

12. The more places you can place yourself online, the more chances you have to show in search results.

13. The more original, quality content you create, the more chances you have to show in search results. Google will begin to see you have a niche and will show your business when someone is looking for your niche.

14. The more domain names you have pointing to your main website, the more you may show up on searches.

15. The longer you've owned your domain name as well as how many years it's registered into the future may increase ranking. Google may see a website as more solid the longer it's been around and the longer it's pre-paid into the future.

16. Do some competition research. As a small business, you should frequently search your most used keywords and see what pops up. If a main competitor in your area is always coming ahead of you in the listings, click around their website to see what might be the cause. Sometimes they have a business and domain name that's been around longer and they've built lots of content on their website. If you think you can't show up on searches above them for the same keyword searches, try and make yourself a niche using a different keyword. Keep at the social media, video making, and content building until your organic rankings raise. Realistically, if your business shows in the top three on searches, you have the best chance of customers clicking on your business. Get to that top three!

> Do some competition research using your most used keywords and see what results come up.

17. Google relies partially on prominence to rank listings. Your website may be more prominent than another

website because you have more involvement across the web. Links, articles, directories and more reviews and positive ratings than other businesses may make Google rank you higher.

18. Make sure your Google My Business page is filled our completely. Google favors those over incomplete ones.

19. Get listed in local business directories. It's easier to focus your marketing strategy locally than trying to compete online with businesses nationally or globally. You could use your local newspaper, Chamber of Commerce, or visitor's center page to list your business. If you're on their website, that's another external link for you.

20. Are your page titles, Meta tags, and Alt tags all filled out for each page and picture on your website? Search engines want to bring readers to the content they are searching. The better your keywords and descriptions the better your potential customers can find you. A common mistake is forgetting to fill these areas out on parts of your website. Double check that all pages of your website have these filled out.

For years, when I typed Massage La Mesa in the search bar the first 5 listings were all to my business from different sources. But the cool thing was any one of those five were my business, so no matter which one someone clicked on, they were going to contact me.

- There was a Google listing for Massagelamesa.com.
- Then came a listing for our Yelp page.
- A listing for our Facebook page.
- Then either our marketing page on sports massage or a blog post showed up.
- And our LinkedIn page often showed.

Local Listings

If your business is targeting local customers, then local listings are important for you. We've already mentioned having your name, physical address, and phone number on every page of your website. Also making sure this information is consistent throughout all your online presence is key. Google wants to see Allison Avenue spelled out if that's how you wrote it on your website. Avoid putting Allison Ave. on other online sites, as this muddles the search engines. You will want to focus on keywords with your city name, nearby zip codes, and nearby city names. Businesses near yours that mention you online helps with your local listings as well. There are companies you can hire to increase your local listing online.

Organic listings will come over time. If you work diligently on different online listings, your website will gain a larger footprint. Steady additions to your online presence are better than a sprint to dump it all online at once. Find your niche in the keywords related to your business and create quality content on your website, blog, and the social media you chose. Organic listings are worth your time because the customer came to your business when they were looking for something they needed. These customers are more likely to become long-term customers and return when they have a good experience.

ACTIVITY: Use this chapter as a checklist to get all the pieces of the SEO puzzle completed over time. Start with your website pages and tags, and check them off when it's done. Pick another item, and check it off. Take one piece at a time, and the whole puzzle will be completed soon enough!

Notes and Research

CHAPTER FIFTEEN CHECKLIST

☐ Complete the activity for this chapter.

☐ List your website profile on a Google business page.

☐ Add social media sites.

☐ Getting reviews will give customers the information they need to choose.

☐ Write articles for professional publications to gain a link to your website.

☐ Get your business named online using a press release.

☐ Donate product to another business in exchange for naming your business.

☐ Partner with a complementary business teaching a class.

☐ Network with other small business professionals to share referrals.

☐ Use keywords for blogs on your website.

☐ Get testimonials from clients to share online.

☐ Make videos with keywords in the descriptions.

☐ The more times you place yourself online, the more chances you have to show in search results.

- ☐ Create original, quality content to have a better chance of being found through Google.

- ☐ Point multiple domain names to your main website for better chance on searches.

- ☐ It is thought that the longer you've owned your domain name as well as how many years it's registered into the future may increase ranking.

- ☐ Frequently search your most used keywords and see what competition pops up.

- ☐ Google relies partially on prominence to rank listings.

- ☐ Don't leave anything blank on your Google My Business listing.

- ☐ Get listed in local business directories.

- ☐ Fill out all page titles, Meta tags and Alt tags for each page and picture on your website.

Chapter 16
Paid Advertising

There are paid options for boosting the chances people come across your website online. If you find yourself with a budget to devote to online marketing, you might to try one of these.

Pay-per-click

Pay per click (PPC) is a way to drive traffic to your website when an online viewer sees your ad and clicks on it. I found it was manageable for all budgets because you only pay when they click, and you can set a limit on the dollar amount you want to spend. With that in mind, if you don't have a lot to spend, you may want to narrow your niche or keywords as small as possible to gain the most quality leads you can. The goal here is to turn the "click" into a sale. If you pay for quality over quantity, you have a better chance of a viewer being interested in a specific niche your business offers, and hopefully your website does the rest.

If I love working with pregnant women and supporting them through their pregnancy with massage therapy, I might use pay-per-click advertising to focus on bringing those clients to my website or a landing page on my website about prenatal massage. From there, the viewer can read more and hopefully book an appointment. If my goal is getting them to book an appointment, then they better live near my office.

In Facebook ads, as you set up your pay-per-click account, you can put in the demographics of your target audience. So, I may choose a 10-mile radius surrounding my office. If you are an online based company that makes fitness products for triathletes, then your pay-per-click would target different key words than mine for prenatal massage. You also don't need your ads to show to local people exclusively because your ship your product.

Google ads

Google ads are what most people think about when they hear pay-per-click. Your business will pay $1-$2 per click when using this platform, and it can get very costly if you leave your keywords too broad. We know the paid ads are placed at the top of the page like you see in the example below. In this Google search I typed "Google ad manager." As you can see on the left side of the page, the first two listings have **Ad** before the website of the advertiser. Google itself is the first one and wordstream.com is the second one. After that, the organic listings begin. Whichever ad I click will be the business that gets charged for the click.

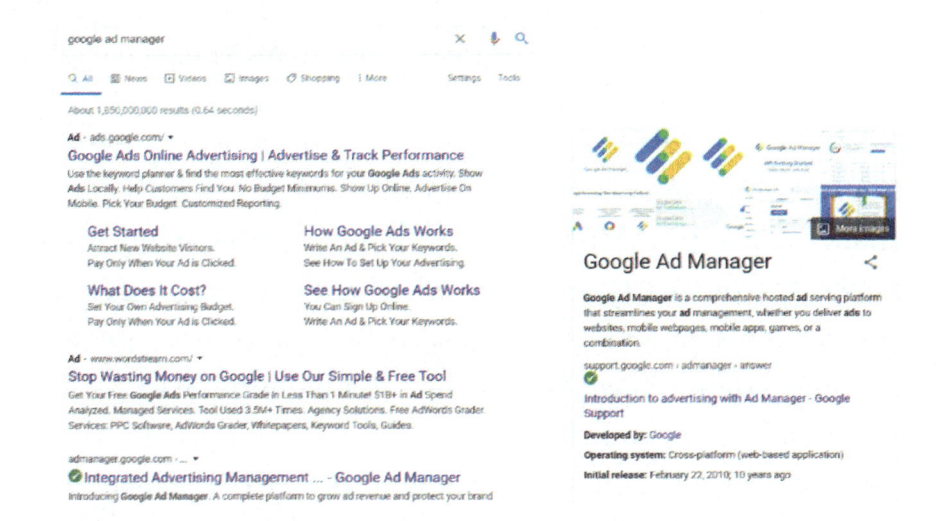

Google ad manager will take you step-by-step through the process of creating an ad for your business. Think of Google ads as a way to bring you new customers based on the keywords or phrase they are searching. Facebook is used in a slightly different way.

Facebook ads

Facebook costs somewhere between $0.27 - $0.97 per click. Facebook helps create your ad with the Ad Manager (Meta Business Suite) tool and is relatively simple to set up. After deciding on your key words or phrases, you'll add text and a picture, and don't forget a call to action. Know what your desired outcome is from the ad. Do you want more likes? Do you want to say "call now" or "book now?" Have a link directly to the place you want to send them. For example, if your triathlete company made a new swim goggle and you want to target sales for that item, you would send viewers to a landing page telling them why they should try your goggles.

> Facebook owns Instagram, so Ad Manager can be used for both.

Eye catching photos work best! With these ads, you have one chance to get the person to click on your business. In my experience, the picture is the key to whether they click or pass up your ad. If it's unique, shocking, or really cool and eye catching, it works. I didn't have the time or equipment to take my own standout photos, so I chose to purchase ones to use for these pay-per-click ads as long as I thought they were good enough to make viewers stop and look.

Run two ads and see which preforms better (split testing). This was good advice I got from an experienced marketer. On Facebook, I ran two ads with the same focus. In this instance, it was sports massage. I tested which one received more clicks and discarded the one that didn't perform as well. I used two different pictures but the same call to action and same general verbiage in both ads. Facebook has built in metrics that record your views and clicks for you to see when you log in to your account. You can also see how much money you've spent so far and how many days are left in the campaign. If you're an information junkie like me, this is fun to check and see your progress.

Below is a picture that performed well for me.

Remember, don't write your ad before you know who you're targeting and your desired outcome. If you are going to make the most out of your money, you need a clear understanding of your goals and expectations. Also, following the success or lack of success is important so you can move on to another form of marketing if PPC isn't working for you. Another option is hiring a PPC professional for help.

When it Might Make the Most Sense to Use PPC Advertising

We've discussed other forms of marketing like Search Engine Optimization. PPC can complement SEO in filling the time it takes to have SEO working well and driving a steady stream of traffic to your website. A PPC ad can drive immediate traffic to your site and help you gain recognition more quickly.

You may use PPC to bring awareness about a new product or service to your company. In case your product doesn't fall under an easily searched category, you can use PPC to funnel your target audience to your product. Remember the triathlete goggles? What if your new product wasn't something triathletes already knew about? You can still set your ad for the new item to target triathletes, and it will show up to people who are interested in the sport of triathlon who ideally will find it something they can't live without and click to purchase.

Another reason you may want to use PPC is to get your name in front of competitors who have a better online presence. As you are starting, the reputation and name of your business is building, and it's not realistic that your website will show above long-standing websites in the search results. This means that while you are working to gain noticeability organically, you can buy visibility for keywords where your well-known competitors currently have an advantage.

The key is to use pay-per-click advertising wisely because as soon as your budget is spent, your ad disappears. There will always be a bigger company with more money to spend, so make those ads as specific as you can to bring high quality leads. The main difference between Google ads and Facebook ads is Google helps you find new customers while Facebook helps new customers find you. Now you know the basics when you are ready to dive into this area of building your business.

ACTIVITY: Begin to notice the ads that catch your eye on social media. What is it about them that makes you take notice? Realizing someone has paid for that ad to show up on your feed, do you find it effective? Does it make you want to take action? By bringing your awareness to these areas now, you will write better ads when you are ready to pay for advertising.

Notes and Research

CHAPTER SIXTEEN CHECKLIST

☐ Complete the activity for this chapter.

☐ Notice which type of ads make you stop and read. Do colorful pictures make you stop and take notice or is it the image of the picture?

☐ Identify your budget, if any, to pay for advertising. Decide when in the future you will be ready to pay for advertising.

☐ Decide if Google ads or Facebook ads would be more effective for finding your ideal clients.

☐ Look into s courses you can take to learn ad writing yourself.

Chapter 17
When to hire a professional

This journey of building your website can be overwhelming at times. I know you have the courage, or you wouldn't have started your own business. Your entrepreneur mind, in all its wisdom, will know when you need to hire the help of a professional. If you reach a step in this book that has you banging your head against the wall, hire a professional. It's like taxes for me. For many years my business was small enough I could do my own taxes, but it was something I seriously disliked. I could do it myself, but why should I when it caused me mental and emotional stress? I decided to hire a professional to take it over for me. It's one of the business decisions I made and I shouldn't have waited so long to do it. Here are the best places to pay a professional and why.

Logo

A professional-looking logo says a lot about your company. Finding something that reflects your business can be challenging. There are different styles of logos, and one may represent your business better than other styles. I have seen people design their own logo, but I caution you in this. Unless you have prior graphic arts experience, it is extremely difficult to create a professional looking logo in all the formats you will need and for the variety of uses necessary.

For example, the format for online use of your logo is different than the print format for your business card. The social media format has square dimensions where your original logo may be rectangular. There is a scalable logo in vector format to be used in huge prints like a banner on the side of a building or for your table at an event. You can create a semi-custom logo with online companies which will come in most of the formats you will need. The downside to this is you are extremely limited in the logo design while the upside is that it's inexpensive. It's going to depend on what you want, but in my opinion, when it comes to designing your logo, there is good reason to pay a professional.

> Hire a professional if you get stuck or are stressing more than advancing your website.

Keyword research

There are tools to carry out the keyword research which you will use in multiple places for marketing. We've talked about keywords being used on pages of your website and blog, and when you write descriptions for social media posts and videos. You may want to hire a professional to do keywords for you if your time is better spent elsewhere or if you want more in-depth results. Obviously, a professional has more experience and insight. Sometimes while building your business, you have to know where your skills are best used and get help where they are weaker. I found the keyword tools are good to get an idea of the main keywords you will want to use, but there may come a time where a professional can benefit you more. If you've been in business for a while and are ready to re-evaluate keywords, hiring someone is nice. They do the leg work and present you with the list of words plus statistics of the competition for those words. As your industry changes, the most searched keywords will too. Some industries change quickly (every 3 months) and others you can re-evaluate every 6-12 months.

SEO optimization

Title tags, Meta tags, Alt tags. SEO is an area where you will likely want help eventually. It is such an in-depth, everchanging world that there is no way we as small business owners can know as much as a professional in this area. This book presents the very basics of SEO to introduce you to what it's all about and as a business owner you should gain as much knowledge in this area as you can. There is enough information here to get started using the SEO tools the builder will have for you. Think about hiring a SEO specialist some time after the first year of having your website up if not sooner.

Social media

You may be a rock star at social media and never need to hire a professional. The following points are for the people who get a headache keeping up with posting on social media. Fact: there are many, many social media sites that may help your business. Fact: each site has different ideal frequencies for posting content. Fact: each post needs keywords. Fact: consistency is success in social media.

As a business owner with so many tasks to run your company day to day, it can be difficult to keep up with the social media posts. If you don't put a system in place, weeks go by without a post on one or more platforms and then your social media isn't really doing its job marketing your business. Is it better to do a few social media sites mediocre or pick a couple and do them well? Do one or two well!

Don't let time go by without posts because you can't think of something. There are helpful tools you can get that take one post and re-post it on multiple platforms and that saves time. If social media is the nagging task always in the back of your mind it may be worth the cost to hand that area over to a professional. They do it every day and are experts at getting the results your company needs.

Assessing your website

This is an overall assessment of how well you built your website. The professional will look at everything from layout and navigation, to finding dead links, to keyword usage and the tags you put on each page. It's similar to a proofreader for your website. The value is their expertise in knowing when a keyword is used too frequently or in the wrong place. Or maybe you thought you added an alt tag to all your pictures but they find a few that got skipped somehow. Paying a professional to put their eyes on your website and give you suggestions for changes or improvements is highly recommended within the first 6 months of publishing your website. The sooner the better. You can always do some of the corrections yourself and pay the professional to do others if they are beyond your knowledge base.

ACTIVITY: You may do all the steps for building and marketing your website yourself. You may hire someone to help you here and there. Any mistakes you make can be fixed, so don't be afraid to learn as you go. Keep your focus where it matters which is generating business for your company. Price some professional services and have their number handy in case they are needed.

Notes and Research

CHAPTER SEVENTEEN CHECKLIST

- [ ] Complete the activity for this chapter.

- [ ] Is there any part of website building or marketing you strongly dislike or can't do? How important is that part to your business right now?

- [ ] Decide if you can allocate money from the budget to hire a professional

- [ ] Free resources in your community like SCORE offer trainings to learn how to do some of these business tasks.

- [ ] Online courses teach all areas of website improvement.

- [ ] Work to advance and improve your website constantly.

I hope you are successful in your DIY website and getting found online. It will look professional and bring new business to you all hours of the day. This book has all the basics so keep it handy to refer back to certain chapters as needed. Good luck and have fun. You got this!

Made in the USA
Columbia, SC
23 August 2022